Happy Policeman

Moments in Life

Attention Authors

'We Convert Fighters into Writers'. That has been the motto of Manas Publications, since more than four decades. Our message to the world is that India can win the battle, not only by bullet but also by the pen. There is no dearth of intellectuals in our country, but their knowledge is confined to them only. No sincere effort has been made by any other publisher to channelise their knowledge in national interest. That is why the talent of a large number of intellectuals, remains latent. An author transforms his knowledge into a manuscript, and it is our job to spread his/her knowledge by converting it into a beautiful book.

For over four decades, Manas has been motivating the intellectuals by publishing their manuscripts and would like to publish your manuscript too. If you or your colleagues have any manuscript ready for publication or are working on it, kindly contact us with detailed synopsis and the list of contents. We would transform your work, into a valuable publication. If you wish, we can also suggest you, the suitable subjects for writing books, related to your area of expertise. Manas is known for its publishing quality and commitments. We take utmost care in production and give wide publicity to the book, as well as its author, through our national and international distribution network.

Happy Policeman

Moments in Life

D.C. Nath, IPS (Retd)
Former Special Director, Intelligence Bureau

Manas Publications
(We Convert Fighters into Writers)
New Delhi-110002 (INDIA)

MANAS PUBLICATIONS
(We convert Fighters into Writers)
(Publishers, Distributors, Importers & Exporters)
4402/5-A, Ansari Road (Opp. HDFC Bank)
Darya Ganj, New Delhi-110 002 (India)
Off. 23260783, 23265523, Res. 23842660
Fax: 011-23272766
E-mail: manaspublications@gmail.com
manaspublications@yahoo.com
Website: www.manaspublications.in

ISBN 978-81-7049-545-1
₹ 495/-

Designed at Innovative Processors

Printed in India at
HS Offset Printer, Delhi and
Published by Mrs Suman Lata for
Manas Publications, 4402/5-A, Ansari Road (Opp. HDFC Bank),
Darya Ganj, New Delhi-110 002 (INDIA)

Foreword

Sri Dhanesh Nath has had 38 years experience in the Intelligence Bureau of the Government of India. He has written a narrative rare to come by. It is primarily his professional autobiography, but it describes as much about how he traversed as a police officer in a variety of job postings as about his colleagues, senior and junior, in the States of West Bengal and Bihar and also in the Central Government. Personal and anecdotal, the narrative is absorbing, sometimes surprising and sometimes amusing. His memory for details is amazing; but the way he describes the events, circumstances, persons and activities vouches for the richness and variety of Sri Nath's experience in his long career as a public servant, often "behind the curtain".

The underlying currents for recognition in this work are the author's patriotism, love for the people with and for whom he worked, dedication and commitment to the responsibilities put on his shoulders from the start as a young officer in the Service. He seems to have earned and enjoyed a warm relationship both with his supporting staff and supervising senior officers in many places he was posted. His cultural interests and associations that find mention in the book, despite the nature of his official work, are noteworthy.

Many young police officers of today will find the book interesting and beneficial to read.

R. Venkatanarayanan IAS (Retd)
Formerly Secretary to Govt. of India
March 24, 2017

Acknowledgements

I have written the book in the office of the Patriot's Forum. This has been possible due to Late Shri D.K. Mittal and then because of his worthy son Shri Deepak Mittal. This book would not have seen the light of the day but for such comfortable, almost a palatial place, allowing me to begin and complete this book. I have no words to express my heart-felt gratitude to Deepak. I am indeed deeply obliged to both of them.

I am indebted to Uma, who worked with me for some time and had shown patience to take out copies of what I had written any number of times without any grumble. I am more deeply grateful to Bandana Kushwaha, who has shown immense patience in taking out copies. I have corrected and revised these copies any number of times. She did not feel irritated and bore with patience till the book has been finalised. I am also grateful to Smt Sunita Tiwari in the office to keep the atmosphere very healthy, happy and sweet.

Sanjeet Kunwar saw to it that things in the office are always in order so that nothing could become any handicap to me. Ramji, office attendant, provided all the material comforts I needed to work in the office. There are a few other office attendants, who also played similar role. Capt (IN) Ratan Syam Chawdhury and Smt Kakoli Saha always enquired how far I had proceeded in writing the book.

I am deeply grateful to Shri Shankrendu Duttamajumdar for having edited the book very meticulously, when he was having lot of personal difficulties.

My gratitude to Shri R.V. Venkatanarayanan knows no bounds. He wrote such a beautiful FOREWORD in very quick time, taking me by surprise.

I am indebted to my publisher who readily agreed to take up the task of publishing the book.

I am greatly indebted to my seniors and juniors, in the West Bengal Police where I had worked seven years, then in the Intelligence Bureau till I superannuated in 1995 and the IISSM, where I had spent almost 14 years and now in the Patriots' Forum who had all helped me to feel happy so as to be able to record the happy moments in my life. How can I not talk about the Alumni Association of the Calcutta Presidency College? The atmosphere in the meetings/get-togethers have been extremely happy and sweet.

The Chanyakya Puri Durga Puja has been a field where I loose myself in happiness undiluted. So, also is my indebtedness to the Matri Mandir and friends thereof with whom I have been brushing shoulders almost every evening.

Preface

This book is kind of personal memoirs of an average policeman turned into an Intelligence Officer and later on spent over fourteen years in the corporate world and now has been working in an NGO having happy moments all the while along with spending happy moments in some social cultural institution.

The book also incorporates my happy brushes with seniors in the services and other friends, especially juniors as also in the corporate world and during the current times.

Since I had not maintained any diary, I had to fall back on my memory, which fortunately did not play any spoilsports. On the other hand, it started haunting me, even when I was in some friend's houses, forcing me to note down the points immediately on return home. In more than one sense, I have enjoyed and had happy moments all through this period, barring six months towards the end of the training period at the CPTC, Mt Abu.

In more than one sense, I have been lucky. For example, I had a chance to go to South Africa (where I am not initially supposed to go) and had the privilege of experiencing South African lions live, on which there is a three hours long CD. Perhaps more than lucky. In order to break the monotony of intelligence, intelligence and intelligence, I have deviated at places. There may have been some repetitions, for which I would beg forgiveness.

I have had the privilege of working under senior bosses, who were known to be hard masters but have been very kind to me. That is God's grace! I am a Bengali (of course I am a proud Indian Hindu) and as such many sentiments common to the Indian Bengali's have come out. In the book, there would be some reference to the Calcutta Presidency College.

I have had the privilege of traveling widely inside the country. I could humbly claim that I have been to all metropolitan capitals, cities and villages. Luck was with me in taking me to places outside India, where I was not supposed to go my own. I have also visited almost all places of Hindu pilgrimage. I could not, however, go to all places.

I do go to Matri Mandir almost every evening and spend some happy moments with friends there. I have been having happy moments in the PF office also. That is my luck holds on.

I had to use the dirty 'I, because it is based on my personal memory'.

D.C. Nath

Contents

Episode-1

I happened to be an accidental Police Officer. My late father was a Judicial Magistrate, not favourably disposed towards the police. While studying in the Presidency College in Calcutta, my ambition was to do Ph.D. in historiography in the University of Columbia. Dr. Amalesh Tripathi, whom we called the Toyenbee of India, had arranged this for me and then to teach in the Presidency College itself.

When the results were out, there was a complete change in the scenario. Dr. Amalesh told me to seek future outside the academic world. He cited the poor pay scale of the teachers and unfortunate politicking in the matter of posting in town colleges or in far off sub-divisional or in rural colleges – thanks to the office of DPI.

In any case, a dream was shattered. When I went home I lied on the floor and was sobbing. My eldest brother, who was like my father, condoled me, "What has happened?" I told him. Dada advised me to do as told by Dr. Tripathi. I do not have any regret over my joining the police and then becoming an intelligence officer. I have highly enjoyed both.

This was Providence, I hope some serving police officers will read the book, which is based on the personal knowledge of a brother officer. The experience narrated will certainly make them better police officers.

I have always held: share your joy, suffer your sad moments silently. Right from the beginning, I have had countless occasions of happy moments – both in my short uniform police career of seven years in West Bengal and then the rest in the Intelligence Bureau of the Government of India. I did not have the habit of maintaining diary. And so, it is possible many happy moments have skipped my mind. I am the looser for that.

I was at the Calcutta Esplanade tram depot waiting for the tram I wanted to board. I heard some youngsters like me saying, "Do you know one Bengali boy Dhanesh Nath is the first among the successful Bengali IPS Officers. He is also the fourth in order of merit in the All-India list. That is good. I know this boy. He is from Kalighat and later studied at the Calcutta Presidency College "We had to join at the IAS training centre, now known as the Lal Bahadur Shastri National Academy of Administration at Mussoorie on the 16th May, 1960. From our batch, probationers of all services were to attend the Foundation Course at this center, located at the old Charleville Hotel. We were about 350 probationers in the first batch. All could not be accommodated at the main Charleville building. I was among the few lucky ones to be at the main building. There was a three bedroom apartment on the first floor. In the front, room was occupied by Ravi Kathpalia, who always beat me in table tennis. Ravi skipped the IAS and chose to join the IAAS so that he could always stay at State Capitals. He was good in tennis also. He was a good commentator. Sarvi, his elder brother, was in the IFS. The ever smiling Promod Kapoor and I shared the middle room and Obed Angami was in the third one. Showing the dozens of bottle on his table, Obed used to say, "This is my food". We really never saw him in the dining hall, Obed had become the Chief Secretary, Nagaland.

The principle of national integration was in full flow in distributing the probationers at the Charleville and at the Happy Valley. The vast majority of the probationers were at the Happy Valley, down below.

We were given initial tips of horse riding near the Happy Valley. There we first learnt, "Make much of your horses", as pronounced by the riding master. We, the IPS probationers, had to pass the riding test at Mount Abu, the Central Police Training College (CPTC).

Dr. A.N. Jha, a scion of the celebrated Jha family from Allahabad and himself a great scholar, who later on became the Lt Governor of Delhi, was the Director at the Academy during our time. He was all wit and humour personified. While the bulk of the probationers were in the classroom, Dr. Jha played fun and frolics with about 20 probationers at the beautiful lawn. Ajay Mitra, known as Lenin, IAAS, was the brightest among all probationers in our batch, he was in Dr. Jha's tutorial. Lenin once asked Dr Jha," Sir, we see you coming to the Academy around 11 am, sit at the lawn, frolicking with a group of probationers, while the classes are on. Shri Dwivedi (who later succeeded Dr. Jha) does all the work. So, Sir, what exactly do you do in the Academy? "Prompt came the repartee, "Well Lenin, have you been on a ship on the high sea? There is the Capt. frolicking with women in the decks. You will find him at the hull only when there is a storm, requiring the Capt. on the wheel. So, the choice is yours." The group got stumped.

We had Salman Haider and Ashok Chatterjee, both had appeared at the combined competitive examination from Oxford. They put on drainpipe trousers and tried to speak with Oxonian accents. Salman, who was later to become Foreign Secretary, was the worst. Once, some of us accompanied Salman to the famous Sardarji's tailoring shop in Kulri. The tailor was busy in satisfying Salman. At one stage, Salman was completely pinned down. We were wondering how would Salman come out. The tailor master took a big size mirror and told Salman, "Sir, we hope it is now alright." Salman's reply was classic. In his affected Oxonian style, Salman said, "Apart from the major defects, it is alright." Needless to add, Salman was in a new trouser by then. We then had our eats at Kulri and rushed to the mess for our dinner. Well, here also was another Salman-like friend He was Khambata. He just could not stand the smell of the food in the mess. Yes, quite justifiably. So, he enjoyed his breakfast. Once, he had at one go finished 19 toasts, liberally pasted with jam and butter. Some of us asked him, "Khambata, why not have one more"? Pat came the classic reply, "Well, I have had 19 toasts. Why be greedy for one more?"

Then the story of Pronobda. Senior to me in age, PK Biswas enjoyed his drinks. We had to often pour bucketful of water on him to bring him back to senses.

Then, Lenin and Raghupati, Raghupati liked my blood-red silken tie. He said. "Well, DC, you have to give me this tie. I had no answer to this innocent friendly request. Lenin and Raghupati were roommates and great friends. Once asked what was his pet aversion, Lenin did not look right or left. He coolly said, "My roommate and cockroaches".

Playing a game of bridge earned friends in Mussoorie. SV Krishnan, IFS and another senior colleague who joined IAS from earstwhile Indian Frontier Administrative Service, and a few others were regulars. Shri P.P. Shrivastava was a regular in the lobby in the evening.

Sankar Sen, IPS, a Calcutta Presidency College senior and Gadadhar Chatterjee, IAS, one year junior to us in Calcutta Presidency College, were in favour of the well-known shorter version of the three card game. Gadadhar, mama's innocent boy, who came to the college in dhoti and kurta, was quick to pick up this shorter version of the game. He used to be heard shouting, "Sankarda, Sankarda, time is money". His conversion was complete.

Annual Durgapuja was an event in Mussoorie for the probationers of Assam, Orissa, West Bengal and Bihar. We obtained permission to visit a Puja, a few miles (9 kms then) away from Mussoorie, in a group of about 30 plus. What bonhomie was that!

Cupid was fairly active in Mussoorie. So, the Academy became a fairly good match maker. Examples galore. The tradition, set at the first Foundation Course, is still kept up, we believe. The matter is too personal to be brought out in the open. All meetings did not, however, end well.

Incidentally, a batchmate of ours Saldanha, allotted Assam cadre, use to entertain us by singing:

"Khoya Khoya Chand, Khula Asaman,
Ankhon Se Akhan Mil Gyi, Tumse Bhi Kaisi Nind Ayegi"

The theme song of the Academy was and quite rightly so:

"If they answer not to thy call, walk alone if they are afraid and cower mutely facing the wall, O thou unlucky one, open thy mind and speak out alone.

If they turn away and desert you when crossing the wilderness,

O thou unlucky one,
Trample the thorns under thy tread,
And along the blood-lined track travel alone.

If they do not hold up the light when the night is troubled with storm,

O thou unlucky one, with the thunder flame of pain ignite thy own heart,

And let it burn alone."(*Shri Rabindranath Thakur*)

Episode-2

From Mussoorie, we went the CPTC (Central Police Training College) at Mt Abu. The CPTC has been the "karmabhumi" of IPS probationers till 1967. If I am not incorrect, the IPS probationers from 1968 onwards joined the NPA. The full name is Sardar Vallabhbhai Patel National Police Academy. The CPTC had made many of us what we have been later in life – a bunch of young men (there were no lady IPS probationers then) who could be differentiated by their look, standing posture and smartness in any gathering. Many among the probationers came, and do even now from the villages and lower middle class families. A look at them at the time of their joining and after the passing out will tell the story.

Our first day at the CPTC was dramatic. Shri G.K. Handoo, an old timer IP and a Kashmiri brahmin by birth, looked every inch like the then British film hero Burt Lancaster, was at the basketball ground. We were sitting on the stairs on one side. Shri Handoo was on the other side across the ground, flanked by Shri E.L. Stracey, a first generation Anglo Indian. We managed to be at the basketball ground by 0940 hrs. That was on October 31, 1960. It was Shri Handoo's last working day in service. We were to meet Shri Handoo there. Everything was set. We had been keenly waiting for something to happen. That is, a friendly welcome address from the Commandant Shri Handoo. But, from the restlessness around, especially on the part of Shri Stracey and Shri Spadigam, the Chief Drill Instructor (CDI), we sensed something wrong.

Well, soon and within minutes, the problem came to the fore. And, it was resolved also dramatically. Four of our batch mates, all turbaned Sikhs, led by over 6ft tall handsome KS Bains, tiptoed and stood behind us. Bains made the move. "Sir, we were under the impression that we were to meet you at 10 am". Shri Handoo thumped the table and boomed, "Impressions? We in the police never believed in impressions".

That was the last we had seen Shri Handoo. Then, it was Shri Stracey for a period of six months. He too was strict but it was really heaven and hell between Shri Handoo and Shri Stracey. Easily, the best possible trainer I have ever seen (and so are the views of many), Shri Stracey was a gentleman to the finger tips. Somehow, I felt, he was very fond of me. I used to be picked up for giving demonstration for a number of difficult physical exercises in front of visitors in place of "ostads", squad trainers, who were Sub-Inspectors of police. My squad was B and our "ostad" was one Prodhan. He too was very proud of me. I had a lot of admiration for him.

An interesting point was the way the squads were formed. This was the responsibility of one Shri Joseph, a handsome tall athlete, who was Asian champion in 200 meters sprint. His job was to form the four squads (ours was a batch of only 43), later coming down to 39 after some friends left for IAS with more or less below in the quality of physical strength.

He asked Sankar Sen (Sankarda) too many questions to identify his physical talents in sports and games. Sankarda, in his college life, did not have any interest in this field. Some of Joseph's questions were, "Do you play football". Sankarda, being a Bengali, answered without battling an eye lid, "Yes, I do". Sankarda felt he had passed the test. Joseph had not done with him. He continued with Sankarda."Do you run"? An easy question. Sankarda, feeling good so far, promptly said, "Yes, I do." Joseph seemed determined to pursue. He asked

Sankarda."What is your timing? "Sankarda now felt cheesed off and decided that enough was enough. He stumped Joseph with a classical answer that Joseph never anticipated, "Well, Sir Joseph, since you are so keen to know, I take my own time. Joseph had no more questions to ask Sankarda. Well, we have many such interesting and highly enjoyable anecdotes with Sankarda.

Shri Stracey occupies a very high place in my esteem. We have seen him holding the post of the Commandant of the CPTC. He used to get the room of the Commandant dusted in his presence every morning, with almost puja like devotion. But, even with all the right, he never for a day sat on the chair of the Commandant.

Once, one among the teaching staff had ticked off a probationer for referring to Shri Stracey as the Deputy Commandant. He was corrected but the honourable member of the teaching staff to took offence have referred to Shri Stracey as the Deputy Commandant. He was officially correct. No sooner this information reached Shri Stracey, he summoned all the IPS probationers, the CBI cadets and all members of the teaching staff at the class room. What followed is a lesson I have never forgotten. Out came Shri Stracey's booming voice, "Friends, I am told one of my colleagues has referred to me as the Commandant of the CPTC." Pointing finger to his chest, he said," I, Shri E L Stracey, am the Deputy Commandant of the CPTC". He repeated this a number of times. He ended up, "I am sorry for all this". The concerned staff was present in the meeting.

Now, Shri Stracey and Sankar Sen. After the morning PT, parade and normally heavy breakfast, it has to be difficult to stay awake in the first morning class. Sankarda devised a technique to stay awake in Shri Stracey's class at least. Shri Stracey was teaching the extremely dry subject of police procedure. Sankarda deliberately sat on the first row to keep himself awake and alert. Despite all efforts, Sankarda dozed off. Shri Stracey, "Sen, I think you need a wash". Sankarda's slumber was broken. He stood up and said, "Yes, Sir!" and walked off. He never returned to the class.

The first great thing Shri Stracey did for the probationers were to cut down the totally unnecessary expenditure incurred by the probationers. Shri Handoo was fond of pomp and show. He got the probationers a ceremonial dress, required to be put on only for the dinner on the passing out night. It cost over thousand rupees those days when our monthly salary was Rs. 400/. Ours was the first batch when our pay was raised to Rs. 400/ from Rs.350/. Like that, Shri Stracey, ensured that our monthly mess bill was within our means. As a matter of fact, thanks Subu, alloted to Assam cadre (later on became DGP of the State. I had met him then. Subu also looked me up once in Calcutta, where I was then the Joint Director, SIB, Calcutta). He has managed to save money even helped us when needed.

Let me add here a small anecdote lest you feel bored. Shri Stracey, though tried to keep a profile of strict and stiff upper lip, had a tremendous sense of humour also. On one mess night, Shri Stracey was "forced" to say something as "the after dinner speech". He smartly went to the small stage. He called two probationers to the dais. He asked the mess havaldar to bring a mug and a piece of rope. The mess havaldar was quick. May be he had been briefed earlier. Shri Stracey passed the rope through the handle of the mug. He asked the two probationers to hold the two sides of the rope, he went to one corner of the dais, said like a magician, "Friends, here are three mugs in a row". Shri Stracey quietly stepped down. We burst into loud laughter. The two probationers hid themselves for some time. I do not remember Shri Stracey being called again for after dinner speech (was not).

We had Dr. Saha, teaching us medical jurisprudence. We made fun of him. If someone tried to divert his attention, Dr.

Saha will say, "No, No, Sir, you are a "historical" student, you cannot ask this question". It went on like that. Interestingly some friends had developed skill of sleeping in the classroom with eyes wide open. It is something like driver of trucks on long distance journey. They sleep and drive almost by habit.

We had three teachers for law, namely, Shri R. Deb, Shri Upadhaya and Shri Gandotra. Shri Deb was easily the outstanding teacher. He had risen from the post of prosecuting police Sub-Inspector. Later on retirement, he went to become the Principal of a Law college in Calcutta.

Shri Upadhyay used to put it like this. "How would a judge, sitting under a cool fan know the practical problems the police have to face".

Shri Stracey was a born teacher in all walks of life. One vening, we were at the Rajputana Club. Shri Stracey came with a guest, an elderly person. In order to show respect to the guest, we instinctively came to the "attention" position. Shri Stracey stepped back a little and indicated to us to "stand-at-ease" position, spreading our legs.

Once I was coming back to the mess in the evening from the Naki take side. Suddenly, Shri Stracey was by my side in his car. He indicated to board the car. Not knowing what to do, I was about to enter the rear seat. Shri Stracey opened the left side of front door and asked me to join him. He then told me, "Since I wanted you to join me, I wanted your company. By sitting at the back seat, you were to make me look like your driver". I was not used to the car culture and hence, did not know about all these intricacies. I apologised. This incident has remained etched in my memory.

Occasionally, on Sundays, we would go to the famous Polo ground to play cricket. It was mostly Shri Stracey versus me. What bonhomie he created through such informal games. Shri Stracey used to be the opening medium pacer. I was wicket-keeper and opening batsman of my team. Rajagopal was the opening bowler from our side. Rajagopal later on went over to the IAS.

We had the privilege of playing cricket with Prakash Naidu, the younger brother of the legendary cricket icon Col. C.K. Naidu. Prakash was an off-spinner.

Once we (IPS Probationers) had an invitation for dinner at the senior officers mess. After the dinner there was the usual relaxation period, a batchmate of ours presented a 'French joke'. We did not understand but went through the motion of laughing. Shri Stracey understood that, then explained the 'French joke' by our batchmate. We then really understood the true meaning of the joke and burst into laughter. The concerned batchmate fled the seen, well before we started leaving for our junior officer's mess.

A few more words on Shri Spadigam, the CDI. He was a terror on the parade ground but outside a very shy man. An excellent trick used by Shri Spadigam was like this. Suppose things were going smoothly. But he wanted to tick off X, he will shout, "You, Nath!" Even though, Nath was not at fault. The entire parade will wake up. Spadigam had some excellent remarks to make, such as, "Don't walk like a pregnant woman."

We had Feida Rasool and batch topper S.V. Trivedi in one room in the mess. Feida was fond of non-vegetarian food. Trivedi was a strict vegetarian with no onion even. They went to Shri Stracey for room changing. Shri Stracey was almost scandalised and said, "What room change? This is national integration". As opposite to this, Mussafir got himself to Bains's room from mine and Sankarda came to stay with me.

We had a room bearer called Ukka, a Rajasthani. Sankarda was getting late for the afternoon class, followed by games. While tying the cades, Sankarda asked Ukka in 'his'Hindi,"*Ghorito deoto*". Ukka was dumbfounded. Sankarda then gesticulated to him, pointing out his fingers to the upper deck of the nearby almirah. Ukka then understood and gave Sankarda his watch. But, then came out Ukka, "Sir, *mere hath se bohut saab pass kiya hay, jeise Angrej, Sardarji etc. aap jo bhi bolieyga bolieye. Bangali or our even Angreji me. Lekin, Hindi me mat bolieyega. Abhi dopohrko tin baje mai ghori (mare) kahanse leke aunga*?" We were stumped. It was real hilarious.

Once we had a press team visiting the CPTC. We were in the dining hall. After dinner, we had that system of holding the toast for the visiting guests. The toasting was done with simple water. It was difficult to make the press friends believe that we do this drill regularly with water. Mt. Abu was after all a dry place. The visiting friends were insistent we do "that" with the "real" stuff and now we were doing so only to impress them.

Developing personality was like a drill. There were two covered box with some slips. Some subjects were written in the slips. You go up and pick a slip. You have to speak in favour of the subject written in the slip picked up by you and then answer questions for one minute. The subjects were like, "Why do I love to fall from a horse", "Why do I love CDI?". The first two minutes appeared longer than two hours. Fortunately, here was no pass or fail in this test.

Evening in the mess was highly enjoyable. Some of us were almost card addicts. We played bridge generally but, occasionally we played rummy. Sailen (MP Cadre) was a regular like me.

I enjoyed the monsoon in Abu very much. I would put on the gum boot and with the raincoat on, I went up to the sunset point, stay there for some time and then slowly returned.

We went out occasionally in groups. Padmanabhan (Maharashtra cadre) was a great enthusiast in this regard.

We were the 13th batch of IPS probationers. But my room no, which was 13 was rubbed off to make it 12A.

My days of happiness at Mt. Abu came to an end with the arrival of Shri B.B. Chatterjee, the discredited IG of Delhi Police. He was shunted out as a punishment.

Somehow, I fell in the bad eyes of him for the simple reason that I too was a Bengali. In his "misguided" mission to prove that he was not partial to me, he virtually started an almost well-planned programme of discrediting me. B.K. Chaudhary, a tough Jat from Haryana was virtually a self-made man. He was extremely industrious. Chaudhary later on joined the IB and spent some years there. Chaudhary was the best cadet of our batch.

With no aspersion on him or without any sense of envy, the point was he was to be made the best cadet. He got 48 in drill; I too scored 48 in drill. I was easily the best in PT but the PT prize had to be given to a CBI cadet Agnihotri. I was chosen over Chaudhary to command the first march past drill at the polo ground. I was by common consent the best all-rounder in sports but that prize had to go to Paddikal who was good only in distance running. I was the best athlete but that prize had to go to Padmanabhan. When I was doing well in sports, Shri Banerjee told me in Bengali." You are doing so well in everything". He could not prevent me from winning the Tong Cup for the best long jumper of the year. I had jumped 20'2" inches. That was no mean feat. I knew rowing. Nobody else in the batch knew that. I taught rowing to my batchmates. I was the Chairman of a Syndicate study group (selected before Shri Banerjee came).He knew I had written the final paper. Shri Banerjee commented, "it was a heavy paper", commenting on the language of the paper but no suggestions for improvement were offered. Incidentally, this paper was highly appreciated by a giant of a police officer, namely, Shri K.F. Rustamji , later in a different context.

There was small hillock a little away from Mt. Abu. While others would climb up steadily, I ran up to the top in one go, and in one breath. I suspect I have an enlarged heart because of such excessive exertions since thereafter also.

At the CPTC, we went on night check of the Guard between 12 pm and 4 am. We requested Shri Stracey if those on such night patrol could be excused from the morning PT and parade in the morning. Shri Stracey said, "This is our plan to make you tough and so the question of being excused from checking the Guard between 12 pm and 4 am did not arise.

This did indeed make us realise the importance of working under the conditions of stresses and strains in later life.

Before I end the episodes of our training at the CPTC (Mt. Abu) it would not be correct if I did not mention about my reading of Dostovoeski Novel "BROTHERS KARAMAZOV" considered to be the best novel of the twentieth century. Some where in middle of the book, it relished (I wish I had still retained my book), "Suffer: Die Suffer: Die Suffer You must suffer, die you who must die. Suffer, Die you who must Die. But be a man". It is, as if you are not left with any alternative. When about 200 pages of the book left, I was not in hurry or in a mood to complete my reading of the book as if I would loose something of importance.

How can the Mt. Abu episode end without a reference to the famous Dilwara temple, a little outside of Mt. Abu? What intricate design on white stones? This is the only one of its kind.

Since I do not want to talk much on Shri Banerjee's time. We want to close this chapter of Mt. Abu here.

Episode-3

Now after Mt. Abu, over to the State Police Training College, West Bengal, at Barrackpore. The stay there has been enjoyable. Shri B.C. Roy was in charge, that is, the Director, PTC. He was extremely fond of horse riding and a great cook also. Shri B.K. Saha was my room-mate at the PTC. A great friend, BK died young in service. It has been a personal loss for me as well as for other batchmates from all over the country. Any of them visiting Calcutta, had just to tell BK about his visit and the rest was done. BK is remembered as a very successful Commissioner of Police, Calcutta. Once when he had moved out there was a great law and order problem over a football match in Salt Lake Stadium. Shri Jyoti Basu, then the Chief Minister of West Bengal, enquired, "Where is BK"? When apprised duly, the CM said, "I do not know all that. Get BK here immediately". And, BK was there and did what he used to best. The other batch mates were Subhas Gossain, Pronabda (all known from Mussoorie days (P.K. Biswas) and Binayak Bhattacharjee (Binayakda). Both Pronabda and Binayakda have also left this world.

For the first day morning parade, we were told to go in riding kits. We were there in time. We had left riding about six months before the passing out parade. Shri B.C. Roy came on horseback and asked us to follow him. He took us all over the PTC area again and again. Having been unused to riding for a long time, the legs started aching. Possibly, Shri Roy sensed that and did not want to give us any relief. He was, however, not a saddist by any means.

One of the first things, we did on joining the PTC was to call on Shri A.K. Pal, the senior most Commandant of an armed police battalion. The orderly received us in and told us to take our seats, adding that Sir would soon come. In came Shri Pal. We stood up and remained in attention. Asking us to sit down and feel comfortable, Shri Pal stunned us, "Do not work. See, I work hard and so all work comes to me. There are many who idle away their time, "Shri Pal was indeed an affable and friendly senior. We met him several times during our stay at the PTC.

We were soon to go for Survey Training for three weeks. Shri B.C. Roy sent for me and gave some money. He said, "I know you people are in need of money. Share this with your batch mates. Return the money when you receive your salary." Well, that was indeed a great gesture by him. I remember that by the time we came back to the PTC, we got some money. I purchased an Omega watch in Calcutta for Rs 600/ odd rupees. I understand that watch is now worth some lakhs.

During the Land Survey training, we stayed in tents. We had the privilege of meeting a grand old man, Shri Batakrishnababu (possibly Bata Krishna Dey). He was an institution by himself. He taught us land measurement with practical exercise on khatian. Batakrishnababu once narrated, "Being the senior most government servant in a mouza, I was approached by the locals to preside over the Rabindra Jayanti. They were insistent despite my strong protest. They took me to the place of the function. I sat with a grave and serious face. When the call came, I stood up and started speaking". What Batakrisnababu said is a long story. Briefly, after saying that Rabindranath Thakur was after all a son of the soil as such he was matir chhele). And thus, once he was on mati, Batakrisnababu went on for an hour or so on how khatian was made and was highly useful. Well done, Batakrishnababu.

I am sure this process would go on and on so long as Batakrishnababu would be there at this mouza or that mouza.

One evening, we were at the mess, just gossiping. We all five IPS probationers and four direct recruit State probationary Dy SPs and some more Customs/Excise Assistant Commissioners. One Shri Sen looked after the uniform requirements. Pronabda hardly talked and normally sat quiet. But, when he talked, that was hilarious. Shri Sen had a shining bald head with not a single speck of hair. Pronabda suddenly said, "Sen babu, what hair oil you use". Before the embarrassed Senbabu could answer, Pronabda clarifed, "Na Na, Senbabu! I just wanted to know the brand so that we can avoid using that brand". We all burst into laughter. Another round of tea was ordered.

Asit, a direct State Dy SP and myself became very good friends. Asit had an excellent habit. When asked, "How are you"?. Asit had the unique response. Raising both the arms up, Asit would politely say,"*Anande aachhi*". There is no way to translate these words. May be "I am in perpetual peace and would carry this forward".

From the PTC, we were sent to different districts for gaining practical experience in the general elections of 1962.I had gone to Serampur to be with Shri Bikash Kali Basu. One fine morning, the range DIG Shri Masood came for briefing the officers. He came. I received him and saluted. He asked my name. I said, "D C Nath". He retorted, "That is not the name. Those were only initials." I corrected myself. He then enquired where i hailed from. When I said "Commilla", all formalities were gone in a trice. Shri Masood came forward and held me close to his chest, warmly for quite some time. I was from his home district. He said, "*Heida na aage Koiba* - The bond created then lasted till this illustrious officer literally breathed his last. That will come later in the book.

Episode-4

In the course of our settlement training, we had been sent to Gangtok, Sikkim. The future king Prince Namgyal offered us drinks. He himself was so much addicted to drinking that he could not keep his eye open and blinked continuously. It was treat to see how drinks are served at that level. There were different smaller branded glasses for different brands of drinks. The Prince had married Miss Hope Cook, believed to have been a CIA plant.

Shri G.K. Balani, IPS, was the Indian Advisor. I was a student of history. And, perhaps made history of sorts in IB. It also so happened I had been fortuitously associated with men who created history or I had been associated with certain developments of sorts that could be called history. I had the opportunity to have been associated with Shri P.D. Malaviya, who created the BPR&D. That has definitely been making history. In view of my background in Industrial Security work and conducting IS training courses, I was deeply involved in the preparation of the PSAR Act. From the IB, we had got the MHA order issued on Public Sector Undertakings not recruiting security guards from foreign security companies.

Episode-5

From the PTC to the thana attachment. I was attached to the Mal Bazar Police Station. It was an excellent place. The Mal thana is earmarked for ASPs training. One Dhirenbabu, a direct recruit Sub-Inspector, was the Officer-in-Charge. He appeared to be a good officer. Well, he must have been. Otherwise, Shri Nirupom Som, SP, Jalpaiguri, would not have sent a trainee ASP under him. More on Shri Nirupom Som later. Whatever policeman I have become in life, it is because of him.

I lived at the police station, except for the night sleep and taking food. It was indeed a rich experience at the P S. Dhirenbabu took care to explain every tit bits. While at the PS, I took the opportunity to read the Inspection Book over and over again. Some of the old-timer British officers, passing by, had left excellent comments. I almost memorised some of those comments, both for professional learning and also for sheer beauty of the style of English writing, full of wit and humour. That stood me in great stead.

Dhirenbabu took me out with him in investigation, in night patrol etc. In the evenings, I played volley ball with the men and officers.

The first month of thana attachment was primarily for training. In the second month, you hold charge of the thana, with the O/C helping you when needed. One could get a good view across the road of the art of plucking the three leaves and a bud and putting those in the basket at the bag. The best tea is atum flush. It should rain during the night and rise in the morning in order that brought sunshine would help growth of tea leaves and bud.

While at Mal, one incident gave me an exposure to know something about Shri Nirupom Som, SP, Jalpaiguri. It was October 21, 1962. The Chinese had attacked us. All gazetted officers of the district were summoned at the office darbar of Shri A.K. Mukherjee, the Deputy Commissioner (District Magistrate) of Jalpaiguri. One incident showed the mettle Shri Som was made of. Every gazetted officer was given supervisory charge of certain areas as premptory measure against the railway bridge or other important road bridges. I too was given some charge. I felt elated and charged up. When everything was over and only Mr. Mukherjee, Shri Som and myself were left, Shri Mukherjee was a real chain-smoker with about six/seven packs of Capstan cigarettes to the left side of his table. Mr. Mukherjee had the last big puff and said, "Well, Shri Som, that's all for the day. "It was past 2.30 am. Shri Som came forward and said, "Shri Mukherjee, I have something to say". Shri Mukherjee, who had very good knowledge of the topography of the district, started wondering whether he had missed out on any important or vulnerable points in the district. But, Shri Som had something else in mind that nobody had imagined. To my surprise, I was the subject of Shri Som. "Shri Mukherjee, you have given Nath a duty to supervise an area. Nath is now doing his thana attachment. Thana attachment is extremely important. If he misses out this, he will never ever get this opportunity. That will be a great handicap to the growth of his professional career. I shall make some alternate arrangement. if necessary, I shall cover up that myself."

Well, I was seething in rage. I started wondering what lay before me for the rest of the district training much later. While doing uniform police work, later it dawned on me how prophetic was Shri Som.

Episode-6

After thana training, it was attachment with the Circle Inspector for a month. It was at Alipurduar. And, look at my luck. I was attached to an outstanding officer, meticulous in everything he did. He was No 2 in the batch, Gourbabu and me became close friends. Gourbabu stayed alone. He was also a great teacher. The game of bridge brought us closer. More on that later.

Gourbabu was on an investigation of a crime. He did not get any clue. Believing that the perpitrators of the crime always leave some footprints. Following this, Gourbabu sat down under a tree. He was asking every passersby, whether any one had seen the criminals. Not getting any answer from the passersby, he decided to continue to sit down under the tree till he got some clues. For about seven days, Gourbabu did not get any clue. Suddenly, one morning, a boy was passing by and was questioned by Gourbabu. The boy said, "Yes, Sir, I remember to have seen the criminals going towards the East. All of them were from a near by village". The boy took him to the village and identify some of the criminal involved in the crime. Gourbabu felt highly encouraged and called for his staff, they arrested the criminals. It proved how true was the science of criminal investigation! As a young probationery IPS officer, I learnt an excellent lesson. Gourbabu thus made me feel happy.

Shri Prabir Chakraborty was the Sub-Divisional Police Officer (SDPO).

We planned our tour in the manner that Gourbabu, the Sub Divisional Munsif Shri Chakraborty and Krishnan, IAS (1961) and myself, went out on tour together. After the day's work, we played bridge till late in the night. Occasionally, the Chief Engineer, CPWD, of the region joined us. I shall have occasions to come back to Alipurduar later.

Episode-7

Now, the district attachment under Shri Nirupom Som. It was God's boon to me to be with Shri Nirupom Som. Shri Nirupom Som was one rare specimen among officers, who was proficient in all aspects of police work. I got some benefit out of that. Shri Som made sure that I got suitable training in all branches of policing work, such as, SP's office, including accounts, police line, district intelligence branch, district enforcement branch, police prosecution branch in the court. Well, that stood me in great stead even when I left the State for a sort of permanent deputation to the Intelligence Bureau. I kept up interest in police work and that helped me write papers for the annual Police Science Congresses – a great opportunity to augment one's knowledge quotient, travel the country and develop friendship, even with elders.

I was at Jalpaiguri. Sarajit, whom I had met at the PTC, was also there. We played bridge in the house of the Hqrs. Sub-Divisional Officer, whenever we got an opportunity.

Shri Som took me out on night patrol. He parked the jeep at least two miles away and we then walked up in semi-darkness to check the disc patrolling work of the police constables.

Once there was a case of police firing. I accompanied Shri Som. When returning, he told me,"Dhanesh, you are lucky. You got a police firing case during the training period". He was so correct. Practical knowledge of such things gave me a lot of confidence to discuss police functioning at different places.

On conclusion of the district attachment, now the test before the "terror" range DIG Shri Durgagoti Bhattacharjee (D.G. Bhattacharjee). Sarajit and myself were to be tested, I was called in. After some preliminaries, he asked me, "At Mal thana, have you read the Inspection Book?" He fell into my trap so to say. I said, "Yes, Sir " I then named the first page remarks of the British officer who was passing by. I had virtually reproduced the inspection remarks. That was the end of the test. Tea was ordered. This laid down the seeds of a long term affectionate relationship between the two of us. Mrs. Bhattacharjee, a paragon of beauty, was also very kind to me. Let me add here that Shri Bhattacharjee was also an extremely handsome man.

Sarajit was grilled for over an hour and did not have any tea.

Shri Bhattacharjee used to take me during his inspection visits to the districts as a part of training. These were model inspections and I had retained those reports with me for several years for reading them over and again. He divided the inspection over six days for the police lines, SP's office, district intelligence branch, district enforcement branch and the district courts. I used to sit by the side, It had been a great education for me.

Episode-8

I was posted as SDPO, Alipurduar. At APD, I played football regularly with the students of Alipurduar College. Its Principal virtually worshipped Kris (Krishnamurthi), who happened to be the President of the college administrative body. Kris narrated that once in the meeting, the Principal Shri Kar, a Professor of Chemistry, said, "Well, ladies and gentleman, we want to do this in 'memory' of Shri Krishnamurthi, Sir." Kris, an excellent human being, rushed to stop Shri Kar, said, "Please hold on Shri Kar. I am still living in flesh and blood". Shri Kar remained as innocent as before till someone whispered the faux pas committed by him.

Playing football with the college students saved me. I had just returned from tour. I learnt that there was a great commotion on the main road of the town. I put on the shoes, took to the wheels of the jeep, telling Padam, the driver, to go to the PS, opposite my quarter and tell the O/C to reach the spot with force. As the MG road at Bangalore city, APD also has one main road running through the town. A truck filled with boulders had run over a child and crushed it to smithreens. The driver left the truck and fled. The angry public was with "chela kaath", that is, big wooden pieces. They were beating all over the truck and some were planning to put the truck on fire. I had reached the place at that time. I got up on the top of the bonnet and was trying to pacify the crowd. On their demand, I wrote out an assurance–some kind of a promissory note, that we would henceforth put policemen on duty at all crossings. So, some "dramabaji" was going on. As the crowd was swelling, I caught the eyes of some of the college students with whom I played football. They courageously put up a ring around me. Thus, they saved me from an imminent danger. By that time, the officer-in-charge of the town police station arrived with Padam and I got back home. What a pleasant memory of that incident remained with me. The incident taught me a lesson as well. I ought not to have acted in that foolhardy manner. But for those college students, it could have been a much worse situation. I call it: the football saved my life on that day.

Shri Som visited APD for supervising an SR case, required to be supervised by the district SP or the Addl SP. In APD or, for that matter, in North Bengal, the majority of the SR cases necessarily occurred in tea gardens. After visiting the crime scene, we were sitting at the veranda of the tea garden manager's bunglow. The witnesses were brought for being questioned by the SP. After we finished, the garden manager politely requested us for a cup of tea. Shri Som stood up and told. "Today, I have come as the District SP. One day, I shall come as Nirupom Som and have tea" Shri Som put on the peak cap, saluted (that was the mode of saying "namaskar" in uniform) the manager and we left.

We had an old jeep of the Second World War Vintage with the SDPO, APD. Soon, when a new jeep came to the Jalpaiguri Hqrs, Shri Som sent that to me. He said, "In Hqrs, I can manage with an old jeep, because I can get that repaired quickly and so, I am sending the new one to you, "A real leader and elder brother indeed!

My SP Shri Nirupom Som sent advance notice that he would come for inspection of Falakata police station (PS). I took the opportunity to visit Totopara to supervise an SR case. Totos are now fast dwindling with about 100 families left. A forest ranger was killed.One has to go to Totopara on elephant back. The place is deep in forest.

I came back in time to attend the SP's inspection. Shri Som's inspection was on the model of the Range DIG Shri Durgagoti Bhattacharjee. The inspection went on for two days. We stayed at the same Dak Bunglow. On completion of the inspection, Shri Som said, "Hay, Dhanesh, *Kaj sikhechen*". That meant I had learnt work. I shared Shri Som' observation with the O/C of the police station. He made me feel proud of him. And, ***I was the happiest man on earth at that moment.*** To get such a certificate from Shri Som was no mean achievement.

Let me narrate the basis of this observation. On the monthly tour report of Shri Som, there were two comments of the DIG. "Excellent" and "Good". The word "Excellent" was crossed through. We interpreted that the word "Excellent" was the first instinctive reaction. But, the DIG was stingy in his comments. He must have crossed through the word "Excellent" and then made it "Good" on second thought, thinking within himself how could he give "Excellent". We guess what Shri Som had submitted could not have been bettered.

I have many happy moments at Alpurduar. Two of my close friends, Shailesh Kundu and Ujwal Pal Chawdhury had visited me at APD. We would go to Kris' house and played tennis there. I had taken Shailesh and Ujjwal to many places, including the famous Bhutan Ghat. The Britishers were known to select beutiful places. You stay at the forest guest house, carrying your provisions. Shailesh, Ujjwal and me went to Bhutan Ghat. Ujjawl caught me in thoughtful mood. That photograph occupies the first page in my photo album. On way to Bhutan Ghat, we encountered chitas (leopard) aplenty. You will have to be extremely careful if you come across an elephant horde.

Kris was in a bad mood for some time. He was boozing with ram for days. His batchmate (name withheld) ditched him. Kris's driver ran to me. And said that I must look up Kris immediately. I went. I called up his father in Madras. He came and took Kris home.

After Shri Som, Shri Satyabasu had come as the SP Jalpaiguri. Satyada as we used to call him had the excellent habit of extending his hand going round and introducing him self as "I am Satyabasu". Satyada was the man of frail structure but could take spot decisions. On my having raised the issue of paying the men of the Home Guards, he said "Go ahead, I shall speak to the IGP daily". Indeed, one can learn from seniors like Satyada as to how take a bold decision, taking the responsibility on oneself.

Episode-9

After a rural sub-divisional, I was posted as the SDPO Serampore.

I was SDPO Serampore. One evening, I was sitting at Serampore Police Station, chatting with the O/C, Shri Manmatha Chakraborty. Suddenly, the police PBX called me and got me at the PS. I was told that the DIG Membsahib wanted to talk to me. I had clearly forgotten that I had to go to DIG's house. Before I could respond, Sushamadi, Shri Masood's wife said, "*Anek hoyeche. Bari jao.* My man would be reaching your house soon". That meant I went home. The man with food for me would soon reach my house from Hooghly, the DIG Hqrs. Sushamadi was indeed an extremely affectionate lady. She looked after me as her son. I later learnt that Shri Masood had told Sushamadi to send me the food home. "*Chheleta pagole achhe. Kothao kono thanate bose achhe*". What he had said meant that Dhanesh was a mad guy. He must have been sitting at some police station. Incidentally, I went to Hooghly frequently and had played bridge with him.

Shri Manmatha Chakraborty with whom I had been sitting at Serampore PS, was a middle-aged man. He was neither frail nor fat. He was smart. When I had enquired how did he maintain such good health. He said, sir I take my lunch at 3 pm and the dinner at 12 pm in the night. That means he takes lunch and dinner at a fixed time.

The annual Rathajatra at Mahesh, the second in religious stature to the Rathajatra at Puri, we were on duty on the road from 4 am. I put my new peak-cap. Senior officers were to come from the District Headquarters in Hooghly. There was a heavy downpour around 8 am. All of us got completely drenched but we all stood our ground. There was strong sun soon after. Our uniforms got dried up on the body. There was about 5 lakh people (pilgrims). Thanks to the alertness of the policemen and officers, not a single case of theft or molestation took place. I walked up and down. The seniors were highly pleased. Around 10 pm, leaving the skeleton staff on night duty, we gathered at the T-O-P Mahesh for debriefing and reassembling on the occasion of 'ulta" Rath seven days later. At the Top, I stood up on an oil drum. I gave a speech for about 15 minutes, thanking the staff for their extremely good work. As I jumped off the oil drum, the staff shouted, ***"SDPO Sir, Jindabad" "SDPO Sir, Jindabad ". It was definitely the proudest and happiest moment in my uniform career.***

Episode-10

I was duly posted as Addl SP in Hooghly district. This, too was an excellent posting. Soon after I joined, Shri Dip Kumar Sen, normally called Dip Sen, there was a strike in a jute mill. The Congress party wanted the police to arrest four leaders involved in the strike. They believed that the arrest of those four workers would break the morale of the striking workers. Shri Dip Sen did not bother about the requests for this being made by the District Magistrate, the Divisional Commissioner. The Range DIG of Police deliberately called the range SPs' conference away from his Hqrs, Hooghly, to Burdwan. Shri Dip Sen called me to his room. He explained, it was a deliberate move to send him away from Hooghly. He advised me to ensure strict supervision of the police duty at the jute mill. Shri Sen said, "Do not listen to any one, keep me posted and hold your ground". In order to boost my morale, he further added, "I know you can do it". And we did it.

The SP came back duly. One morning, the IGP, Shri Upananda Mukherjee called up the SP on the wireless dictaphone. Shri Dip Sen sent for me. The IGP told "Dip, the Chief Minister is after me. You cannot arrest those four men?" Now, please mark what Shri Dip Sen told the IGP in clear and firm tone, "Sir, you have sent me here as the Superintendent of Police. If we can keep the law and order in the district, why shall we arrest those men? But, if you order this in writing, I shall report compliance". The IGP put down the phone.

Well, could there have been a better of teaching the correct things to the younger service colleagues. I did learn the lesson and followed that up in my entire career. I feel proud to have served under such stalwart in the profession.

Incidentally, Shri Dip Sen was an excellent singer. He died an untimely death in an accident while on leave and he was not using any official facility.

When I joined as Addl SP Hoogly, Shri Masood, known as a master of drill and parade, was the Range DIG. (Soon, thereafter, he was posted as DIG, Presidency Range). He was known to be a master of parade.

I presented to him a parade that started with quick march, passing in front of the DIG. And, when the parade stopped, I presented the parade to him in slow-march, peeling off, on both right and left, in slow-march with the tune of "auld lange syne". The parade duly peeled off and left the parade ground. After that, I went up to the DIG and saluted him with the sword. Shri Masood was in tears and told me *"tumi to aamre kandia dilaa"*. I still remember the tears litterly flowing down the cheeks of Shri Masood.

I recalled my first brush with Shri Masood at the residence of SDPO Serampur.

A few words more on Shri Masood, whom I cannot forget. The affectionate bond developed that day lasted till Shri Masood's death. Sushamadi, his wife, told me when Shri Masood was on death bed at the Calcutta Hospital, Shri Masood, often asked, "Did not Dhanesh come"? Well, my respectful pronaams to the departed soul of late Shri Masood.

We were scheduled to stage a drama written by a famous dramatist, Shri Bimal Kumar Roy, 'Ek Pyala Coffee' I was directing the play. The officer who was scheduled to play the main role, suddenly fell ill. Since I had been directing the play and there was nobody else who could play the role, I played the main role. In that role, I had to smoke a pipe, whereas I had never smoked at all. Thus, we had an excellent and enjoyable social-cultural life in Hooghly.

While working hard, as wanted by my SP Shri Dip Kumar Sen, Shri Sen sang, '*Tobu mone rekho, puraatan prem jodi dhaaka pore jai nobo premo jaale*'. The tune rings in my ears even now.

Incidentally, Shri Sen was a short man. He used to play on the harmonium keeping at the usual place in front of him but towards the end, we saw the harmonium at his chest. When he finally left around 2/2:30 am, we felt the music went out with him.

Episode-11

I was duly posted out as Addl SP Darjeeling. Shri Golak Majumdar, a devoted scholar in English, who possessed a big library, primarily having books on English literature, organised my posting to Darjeeling district, where he was then the SP. Shri Majumdar took fancy of me while we, the probationary IPS ASPs, were posted under him at the Durgapur annual meet of the All India Congress 'Working Committee. I was posted at the Police Control Room and was in close touch with him.

It, however, so happened that by the time I reported for duty in Darjeeling, Shri Majumdar himself got posted out to 24 Pargana district. Shri Majumdar called me up and said, "I shall get you back to be with me. He did so. I was duly posted to the police district of Barrackpore as Addl SP under him. This stint at BKP was all hard work but with very happy moments perhaps too many of them.

The best point of my stay at Darjeeling was like this. We were at the parade ground for some social activities. Shri A P Mukherjee was my SP. He suddenly gave me a piece of paper and said, "Read it and return. "My immediate thought was it must have been a message for some incident in Siliguri and I have to go down there, as per the drill.

But, lo and behold! It was the ACR (annual confidential report) that Shri Mukherjee had written on me. It was all in glowing terms. What a lesson he conveyed to me,

The Range DIG then, Shri R.N. Chatterjee was inspecting the Reserve office, which is the charge of the Addl SP. Picking up a file that I had seen, Shri Chatterjee, asked me, "How do I know you have read the file? "I pointed out that I had cut the word Addl SP in the margin as per the standard practice. Looking at my eyes, he believed me but said, "I am sitting here and so I could ask you. But, normally the files come to my office, "How will I know you have read the file". He then explained, "Instead of cut and sign, please draw lines against some portion or part it and write at least "I agree" if you do not have any points to make".

Then, he said, "Well Dhanesh, if you want to make a mark in life, do, at least one inch more than what the office expects you to do". A shiver went down my spine. I have remembered that and have followed that all through since then.

We had a great social life in Darjeeling. We played bridge or table tennis at the officers' club. At times, it was at the house of Shri Manomay Bhattacharjee, D.M. Bhaskar Ghosh, ADM, would join. We also played at the house of Udaynda, DFO or Shri A. Majumdar, a deputy magistrate. There were a few probationary Asst. Magistrates. They were a lively group. We had two batchmats teaching at Darjeeling Basudeb Thakur and Arati Bhattacharyaji. While visiting their house, I had a peep in a Nepali house. However, dirty the Nepalese may look to beat the cold outside, inside the house it was always spick and span.

On way to Saadaphu and Phalut, there is a place called Tonglu, famous for butter and having a suicide point. We got butter from there.

Down on the plains on the other side of the hills was Mirik, the place for the famous Darjeeling oranges, which were generally rather sweet but small in size. .We got basketful of oranges from Mirik. My wife made full use of this easy availability of oranges. When we had gone to Calcutta, her relations spoke of her pinky-pinky cheeks. In West Bengal police, Shri S.C. Dechowdhury is known as the cleverest police officer ever. He was inspecting Siliguri Police Station. He always spoke loudly. People would crowd around in front of the police station, apprehending something having gone amiss.

Shri Upananda Mukherjee was on the line with Shri Dechowdhury, asking for the measurements of a flat. IG's office had asked for these details. Shri Dechowdhury heard him fully and noted down the details. Towards the end of the conversation, Shri Dechowdhury, we heard him shouting, "Sir, I am unable to understand the problem. Sir, please send me a WT message, I shall reply promptly. "Then, he called up the O/C of the concerned police station and told him about the requirements. He set a deadline about the requirements. Emphasing on the urgency of the case, he advised the O/C should take with him two persons as witnesses, break open the lock of the flat, do the needful, get the witnesses to sign and make a GD entry at the General Diary about the reasons for having done all these.

To buttress this, Shri Dechowdhury talked to Shri Dip Sen, then ASP, Kharagpur, who was in the bathroom. The orderly was told to give the phone to Shri Sen in the bathroom. He knew the telephone had a long wire attached to it. Shri Dechowdhury told Shri Sen to go to the spot, get the details and bring the same to him early in order that he could send his reply to the IGP. He added a condition that he must go there immediately.If he would see Shri Sen well dressed up, he would take it that Shri Sen had not listened to his instructions in letter and spirit, meaning thereby that Shri Sen must visit the spot in his bathroom attire and rush to him.

In any case, the details soon reached Shri Dechowdhury. No sooner the WT message was received, the reply that was already drafted, went stating that the response to the IGP's office memo has already been sent.

All these happened before our eyes like a well-rehearsed drama.

Shri Dechowdhury believed that correspondence was like blood flow in the body. It cannot stop. He would send to SP's office letters received with postdated covering letter with, such as, "To the IGP, refer your office memo No. dated, herewith attached is the report of enquiry into the matter by the SP. The SPs generally got at the most 7 days time to report back.

Shri Maloy Dhar was the son-in-law of Shri Dechowdhry. He stayed with us when he came to join the IB. Over the years, Maloy had developed a style of telling the truth on your face. He will bend his head and with closed eyes go on telling you whatever he would like to tell you. He was a dare devil operation master. Sunanda, his wife, helped him in this. She was a charming lady. She died young.

Shri Masood (then the DIG, Presidency Range) and Sushamadi were at Darjeeling. We had a dinner at SP's house. Shri Masood told the SP Shri Arun Mukherjee, he had an upset stomach and they would come by our house, where my wife Chitra would keep some simple food ready for him. They did come to our house. We then went to the SP's house for the dinner. Well, no wonder this man had enquired about Dhanesh from his death bed.

From Darjeeling, there are two roads to go out of the city. One was via the Siliguri-Teesta road with soft hills, always uncertainty of the road getting blocked because land slides. The other one was via Peshok Road with rows tall 'debdaru' trees. After some portion, the journey was down-hill all the way. The famous Lopchu tea garden lies down-hill on this road. We have been to this garden and witnessed the process of tea making. One needs talk about Makaibari tea sold at Kurseong rail station. Some people are fond of Makaibari tea.

There are few other interesting things to talk about Darjeeling. There are two hill tops, namely, Sandkphhu and Phalut at 12000 ft and 14000 ft. The uphill journey to these two hill tops is fraught with danger. At places, you will have to reverse your jeep only by about six inches. In case you lose control, you go down 4000 ft. We always went there with my driver, Buddhiman. Both at Sandakphu and Phalut, you definitely need sunglass. The majesty of the shining Kunchanjangha will otherwise ruin your eyes.

In winter times, when you drive down from Darjeeling, most of the time, you find yourself above floating clouds below you or at par with you on the right side.

An interesting interlude. On transfer to Darjeeling, I was driving down in my new Ambassador car. I had requested the Dy S P headquarters Shri Pradhan to send down to Siliguri a hill driver. It so happened, the driver who met me at Siliguri had never driven any vehicle other than jeep. He told me, he would be uncomfortable with the thought of driving my Ambassador car. So, I decided to drive up to Darjeeling myself. It was a good experience and I felt happy.

I have been to North Bengal in different capacities, first as a probationer, then as the SDPO, Alipurduar, followed by as the Addl SP, Darjeeling, I sang in praise of the natural physical beauty of North Bengal, such as, the over-flowing mountain fountains (jharnas) and effusive greeness of monsoon in the hills, spending winter full moon night in Darjeeling, when moonlight would hurt your skin. The Tiger Hill, just outside the town, you go there at the sun-rise time. The red-crimson majestic Kunchanjangha may hurt your eyes if you are late.

From the Tiger Hill, you go to a place called Takda. The sunshine never reaches there. The cottage there is covered with greenest shrubs. To spend a night there is the job of a brave heart, even with fire place on throughout. We did stay there for one night. As a matter of fact, I have been to almost all tourist spot in the district of Darjeeling including Lava in this south are Kalighura guat home. If you are a light sleeper, your sleep may be disturbed by the fast-flowing Teesta river down below.

The vintage Toy Train is so slow that a batchmate of mine (R.S. Chopra) lost his patience and walked up the last mile or so. I went down to bring him to my house at the top of a kind of a hill top called Gawada Paahar. We could see the rising Kunchanjangha from my house but not hurting the eyes.

I had spent a lot of time in North Bengal. I was the probationary ASP in Jalpaiguri. I was SDPO, Alipurduar and then I was the Addl SP, Darjeeling.

An highly enjoyable anecdote. Satyada, then SP, Jalpaiguri (I had worked under him as SDPO, APD) and we decided to spend a night at a road side guest house, a little away to the north of Gangtok. This guest house was believed to be haunted. There is a kind of an opening in that guest house through which you can see the crimson top of the Kunchanjangha every morning, whether summer, monsoon, autumn winter or spring sharp at 4 am in reverse cone for about ten minutes. We waited with bated breath and behold, that heavenly spectacle was there. It was divine sight.

We need talk about our meeting the then Prince at Gangtok and about the grandiloquent style of serving drinks. Outside in the palace garden you enjoy walking on about 4″ thick carpet of green grass. This is the 'Sikkim Grass'.It is pleasure to take a stroll on this 'Sikkim Grass'. The Crown Prince had married Miss Hope Cook, believed to be CIA spy.

We had indeed a very enjoyable happy and social life in Darjeeling.

Episode-12

After Darjeeling, I was posted as Addl SP Barrackpore.

We tried an experiment at BKP. It was a difficult one. We believe that had not been done anywhere. We organised urban area resistance groups on the model of village resistance group.

I would stand up on a table and address the people often numbering between 200 and 300. Boyed with the success, we planned a district sammelan at Khardha. The draft letter of invitation was sent to the IGP Shri Uapananda Mukherjee to preside over the function. It read Shri Upananda Mukherjee "will preside". He called me up and very decently said, "Are you ordering to preside?" He explained "It should read, the IGP has 'kindly consented' to preside etc". We learnt. The event was a great success. Shri Mukherjee patted me on the back, It was certainly one of the happy moments in my career. I attended the Annual Police Science Congress at Agartala. Shri B K Roy, IGP, Orissa presided over the event. I read a paper on, "Leadership Crisis In The Police". Shri Roy was rather critcal of the subject. He felt I was too young to say that. The paper generated a lot of interest. It virtually led to a kind of debate. Notwithstanding Shri B.K. Roy's ire, the majority was in favour of the motion, I felt very happy. Leadership crisis exists in the police even now and in more intensive manner, never witnessed before. In the police, it is always a top down approach. Examples galore.

Here is an interesting or a rather unhappy development. In a serious discussion, an idea was mooted that the heads of Central Police Organisation should call on the Union Home Minister. There were not many takers. And, yet some senior police officers were sceptic of the existence of the sad spectale of leadership crisis in the police. I have used the expression "babus". That has come naturally because this expression comes naturally in West Bengal, Patna and Orissa frequently. And, I have spent my uniform police career in those States.

With the Left government in power, the ghero culture suddenly became a nuisance. All district SPs were called for a briefing on the subject. Shri Upananda Mukherjee, the incumbent IGP, Shri Bishtu Bagchi, DIG State IB, briefed us. The IGP asked whether anyone had any doubts on any point. Nobody was ready to ask anything. They were more scared of Shri Bagchi. I stood up. I suggested why we could not suitably brief the government that the gherao was illegal. It amounted to wrongful confinement. Shri Bagchi was unhappy with my rasing the question. The IGP said, "We shall examine the matter". I left the meeting happy.

It was UF regime. I would hold area-wise meetings of Citizens Councils. MPs used to send words to me for being invited to the meetings of these Councils. This was our PR work, just as those urban area resistance groups. On conclusion of the General Elections in 1967, Shri Golak Majumdar, the Senior SP rang up and said sarcastically, "Well, Dhanesh, how is it that there were no incident in your jurisdiction? I answered, Sir, this was perhaps because none of us slept for the last four days and nights". He had no answer.

As a matter of fact, during my one year stay at BKP, there had been not a single case of police firing – thanks to the cooperation of the local SDO and ADM. An incident of police firing took place the day after I had left. 19, Riverside Road was the earmarked house for Addl, SP, Barrackpore. It is a palatial house. It is about 5 minutes from Barrackpore police station.

I had stayed at Serampore as the SDPO. Thus, I had stayed on both sides of the river Hooghly. It is not that everybody gets this opportunity. It would not be correct if we did not talk up 'Swarpata Doi' then available at Kanchrapara rail station. Then that white curd of Habra prepared in burnt mud-built container. It is a wonder of wonder. This curd was so stiff that even when the container was held upside down, not a bit would drop down.

There was a case of rioting and counter rioting in Nawada PS. FIRs were filed by both the Communists and the Congress. Within about a week's time, the IGP Shri Upananda Mukherjee called up and said "Dhanesh, do one thing. Get the charge sheet filed against both the sides quickly. When the Chief Minister would call up, I can say that the case was subjudice.

What in-depth knowledge of police working! There was a case of Muslim widow about to lose her property. Somehow, she came to the police station. I happened to be present there. Although it was a civil matter and the police had nothing to do, we got in touch with all concerned and had the matter sorted out. The widow retained her property. I felt happy. The morale of the story is doing one inch more than what the office demands from you.

I was not at home. A General Manager had sent me "Diwali bhet". This, I later learnt, and is a usual custom. Ram Bahadur, one of the two orderlies and my personal servant Ramesh, removed the gift and kept out till I would come home. On return, I called up the office-in-charge Kharda Police Station and got the gift material sent back.

On my performance Addl SP BKP at some point of time, Shri Upananda Mukherjee had observed, there was scope for improvement in the work of Addl SP. I felt rather bad and hurt at it, especially when I used to be in uniform almost for 20 hours. I sent reply to this observation of the IGP direct to him with a copy to Range DIG who was then Shri Masood. Seeing my report, Shri Masood said, "IG *re rakan lekhata aache*".

When I rather angrily explained that I remain almost 20 hrs in uniform, he appreciated that.

Soon there after Shri Kalyaan Chakrabarty who had replaced Shri Masood had come to inspect my office. I explain to him my style of functioning. Shri Chakrabarty said, "I shall come again". He never came back.

Episode-13

Now, a still better part of my service career.

I came over to the Intelligence Bureau in August, I967and stayed there till my superannuation in January, 2005.

Before I go there, I had gone to call on the IGP before I left the State. Shri Upananda Mukhejee showed me a letter and said, "This is a letter asking for my services in 1964. I did not agree. My thinking is that one should go on deputation like yours only after you gained some experience in field police work". He was so correct indeed! The field does help develop the official personality. Once again His blessings. The field police work did help me in many ways. More on that later.

I have written a book, titled, "**Intelligence Imperatives For India**". This is how I have started the book, "For reasons unknown to me, I have always felt I must do something for my country. Perhaps this need within drove me to the Indian Police Service and subsequently I got into the Intelligence Bureau, where I was till the end of my career. I continued with unprecedented glory thereafter in the corporate world for a little over a decade. The Chairman of the American Society For Industrial Security whom I had never met and he knew me through Newsletters circulated by me, wrote to, "DC, whoever comes from India either knows you or have heard about you".

While the full story of my exceptionally pleasant memory in the IB will virtually be a Mahabharata, I shall try to be very

very selective. I would like to start with what should perhaps come at the end.

The writing of that book also has a history. Some well-wishers "got" it written by me. The then Deputy Prime Minister L.K. Advani formally released the book along with a few others in a spectacular function organised by **The India First Foundation.** The publisher did everything, including indexing. They also gave me Rs.15,000/ for miscellaneous expenses. The Director, IDSA, told the Librarian to give me any number of books at a time on his personal card.

I had been inspired by a small book, written by the then President of India, Dr. A.P.J. Abdul Kalam, namely, "India In 2020". And, so out of reverence for him, I sent a copy of my book, **"Intelligence Imperatives for India**" to him. The wonder of wonders, I received a letter from Dr. Kalam on his official letterhead, stating that he had specially liked Chapter IV and Chapter VI of the book. The letter was addressed, "Dear Shri Nathji" and was signed by him. No other police officers' book had received such distintiction. To me, ***this has been the greatest reward received in my service career.*** The publisher got the forward of the book written by Shri KC Pant, then the Deputy Chairman of the Planning Commission. Shri Pant did not know me nor did I know him. He had read the book thoroughly. This is what he has written "The Business of Intelligence conjures up images of mysterious, perilous activity, shrouded in secrecy, deception and high politics. But only a few can lay claim to knowing its inner workings or dangers. Fewer yet are aware of the back breaking monotony of sifting through masses of reports to unearth that one vital clue that makes the tapestry of an analysis invaluable to policy makers, diplomats, political leaders, scientists, the media and hundreds of other actors who may not even be remotely aware of being recipients of intelligence inputs. The author has brought out in a lucid style the various facets of the fast changing security environment and the role of intelligence in taking suitable measures to protect national interest. I have no doubt that this book would be useful for experts as well as student of national security."

God has His own way. On my being deputed to the Intelligence Bureau, I went to call on the Deputy Director, SIB, Calcutta. I had been deputed under a scheme called "Ear marking" scheme. I believe this has since been scrapped because service jealousy of the IAS friends. They do not have any such scheme in the junior ranks. It is available to them when they become Joint Secretary.

During the course of my meeting with Shri R.K. Mukherjee, the Deputy Director, I gained the impression that I would be posted to the SIB, Calcutta, where a number of vacancies existed.

This was not to happen. On completion of the basic training course, I was posted to the Industrial Security Branch in IB Hqrs. I literally shed tears, when the Deputy Director in charge (Shri Ramanujam, an electronics engineer) told me on face, in my first meeting with him, that he did not want me because I was neither an engineer nor even a science graduate. Shri Ramanujam told the Section Officers to send me the file on Durgapur Steel Plant. In any case, I took up that as challenge. As I was studying file, tears started flowing down my cheaks literally. I hardly knew the difference between the voltage and watage. I studied the subject. I organised an all India Industrial Security Conference of the private sector at the Taj Mansing Hotel at Bombay, in which more than 150 senior Industrial Security practioners had participated. That was the first and last such conference. The net result was I was considered one of the founders of the IS Branch.

Once I was in Bombay in a routine inspection visit. I was informed there had been a case of suspected sabotage at the Taropore Atomic Power Plant and that I should go there, inspect and submit a report on that early. Well, D.C. Nath, an arts graduate, did that. On my Inspection report on Tarapore Atomic Power Plant, Shri K.N. Prasad, one of the IPS officers of the first batch (1948), known for his erudition and also being a thorough professional and a tough task master, told me he had forwarded my report to the government and that it had been highly appreciated.

I had submitted a paper for the annual Police Science Congress at Hyderabad. It was on *"**Redefining Police Duty**"*. It was a concept paper. Shri A.K. Dave, of whom every one used to be scared, observed a "thought provoking paper – a great compliment coming from Shri Dave. As luck would have it, Shri M.M.L. Hooja, then the DIB, was presiding over that Congress. He highly appreciated my paper. It was my first encounter with Shri Hooja, who was a work alcoholic. He took fancy of me. The relationship built then continued. More on that later.

Episode-14

I was AD(L), in Police Branch in IB Hqrs. I happened to be the only AD, having the privilege of being present at an ISGP conference. Shri Hooja needed the services of his advisor on police matters, so to say. One primary agenda was whether the IPS probationers should join the Foundation Course at Mussoorie or should go to Mt Abu straight, as in the past. Shri D Sen, then the Director, CBI, was in favour of the IPS probationers going to Mt. Abu direct. On the other side was Shri K.F. Rustamji, who was in favour of IPS probationer going to the Foundation Course at Mussoorie. In the course of his presentation, Shri D Sen happened to, once, say, "Not that I am opposed to drinking". Before he could proceed further, Shri Rajadhakshaya, a colourful character, IGP for Bangalore, got up from his chair, in which he had sulked and said, "Thank God" and he again sulked into his chair. These were the only two words during the course of the two daylong conference, he had uttered. When Shri Rustamii was making his presentation, DIB (Shri M.M.L. Hooja), indicated to me to go to him. I went. He wanted what we wanted. I supported Shri Rustamji. The motion in favour of that the IPS probationers should go to Mussoorie, was carried.

Perhaps as a reward, DIB invited me to the dinner at his house. This was my first visit to 9, Tughlaq Road house of the DIB as the AD. I have been the only AD to have been invited to such a dinner. It was a remarkable occasion in my life. I cherish the occasion even today.

I had taken over from Shri V.N. Kaul as AD (Q). I reported to him as understudy. He physically lifted me and made me sit on his chair and said,"Understudy, bye, bye". It was Shri Venkatachari, then Section Officer who saved me. Shri Kaul was a workhorse. The Q Branch then was the heaviest desk. Shri Kaul would not agree to divide the desk. He was so correct. The security of the seven sisters in the North East is interlined and so indivisible that there cannot be proper appreciation of the security threat therefrom otherwise. Always pan-chewing, he had his separate pen and paper for his personal work. He fought his legal case himself. Shri Kaul had gone to Rajasthan and retired as the State DGP.

While as AD(Q), I had a tiff with Shri Medhakar on a typical issue. I had written the ACR of my Section Officer (of the Q Branch) Shri Venkatachari and sent up to Shri Medhakar. Shri B.K. Mukherjee was yet to join as my Deputy Director. Shri Medhakar returned the ACR stating that I had written it in rather superlative terms. I sent back the ACR, writing," Sir, I have written what I had thought best. I would be grateful to be, pointed out where I had used superlative terms". That ACR never came to me. Let me add that I was not an obdurate officer. What happened in like this I had just sent up the ACR, what Shri Venkatachari had written on one of his assistance Rajinder Kumar. It was indeed in glowing terms. Having seen that, I decided that I, in my turn,would write the ACR on Shri Venkatachari better than what he had written on Rajinder.

Shri Venkatachari was an exceptionally talented as well as a hard working officer. He was also a self-confident man. In my reckoning, he was better than 80 per cent IPS officers. Having joined the IB in Madras as an IDC, he rose to the post of Deputy Director, by dint of grit, merit and, determination. He also had the gift of memory.

We need to spend some time on Dr.Anand Swarup Gupta, the first Director of the Bureau of Reseach and Development. He was the first IPS officer to obtain Ph.D.His thesis was on "The History of the Indian Police".

We were at Shimla attending the Police Duty Meet. I was AD(L). I suddenly got a message to speak to Shri M.M.L. Hooja,the DIB.I was so familiar to talk to him at any time that I remembered the telephone no of his house even. I called up to be told that Shri Hooja would not be able to come. I requested Dr. Gupta to address the meet. Nobody would believe he was the substitute speaker.

Dr. Gupta had a unique quality. He never asked for a second draft. He believed once you had given a draft to your senior, you must have given your best. He had a beautiful handwritng. In the year 2003, there was a very high jump in the price of petrol. Some of us started going to the office in car pool. Shri K.P. Medhakar, my JD, Shri M.K. Boruah, Shri T.S. Bisht and myself were in the same car pool. It was the turn of Shri Medhakar. I narrated my latest meeting with Shri K.N. Prasad at Calcutta airport. On my courtesy question to him, "How are you Sir?" Shri Prasad said, "I am always on the top". I was taken aback. In the car pool, I narrated this and commented on the haughtiness of Shri Prasad, Shri Boruah reminded, "Dhanesh, your JD is in car. Shri Medhakar did not bother.

Deputy Director (S) Frank Dewars was on a routine inspection visit to somewhere in the Middle East. Those were the days when copies of mail used to be taken out and every page so taken out, were counted and kept on records. The First Secretary, who generally looks after security was accompanying him. At certain point of time, the First Secretary whispred, "Sir on the top of this precaution, you would be happy to know this man does not know English". The moment he finished the 6 feet tall gentleman handling the copying machine growled, "Who says I do not know English". The embarrassment felt by the First Secretary (S) needs no mention.

Shri Frank Dewars was travelling in a first class air conditioned coach which had four births two on each side. At a particular station a young IPS probationer entered the compartment and indicated to Shri Dewars to the upper births.

Shri Dewars was in his usual dhoti and kurta. He did not make any protest and obliged the one-star IPS probationer.

It so happened both the IPS probationer and the Shri Dewars were scheduled to get down at the same railway station. A number of police men led by the district SP were waiting at the platform to receive Shri Dewars who was, as mentioned before in his Dhoti and Kurta. The one-star IPS probationer realised what mistake he had committed. The latter who was in his uniform, saluted ever-smiling Shri Dewars. The said IPS probationer quickly fled the place.

Episode-15

I was then AD in-charge of the NE desk at IB Hqrs. At weekly Friday Conferences, I could pronounce the tribal names, possibly in the tribal manner. I used to be called the Tribal Chief.

At the NE desk, Shri R.D. Pande was my JD. Shri Pande was both visionary and practical teacher. He had been IG Nagaland for umpteen years. I called him my father in office. One fine morning his PS Sahadev came to me with a letter that I had only to sign and issue. I felt angry and ran to Shri Pande and told him angrily, "Sir, you could have told me and then I would have showed draft to you". Shri Pande appreciated my feeling and said, "I know you could have done it that would have taken little time, such as, you would draft and send that to me. And I would then have approved or corrected the draft for you to issue the letter. Would not that have taken more time? Now that I have sent the final letter, you could hereafter issue similar letters when necessary". I learnt my lessons from my father in office, it was a privilege!

One evening, he called me up and said we had to give one page note on the seven sister States of NE by six next morning to the DIB for the Prime Minister. We did not have any DD over me then. I rushed to the office along with my long time PA Shri Rattan Singh. The notes were sent to the control room by 2 am. I was then really the Tribal Chief. I did not need any files. The then DIB Shri Atma Jayaram was highly pleased.

A word about Atma Jayaram. One evening, he called me to his office. He briefed me about the operation we were to launch along with the Research and Analysis Wing of the Cabinet Secretariat. No sooner I had reached back my office, his office called and said the DIB wanted to talk to me again. I was put through to the DIB, Shri Jayaram said, "I am sorry, Nath. I have sent my car to fetch you. Please come again" .I did go. He told me that I had to go out of the country along with Col. Hassanwalia, and before that to go and meet Shri R.N. Kao, the founder Secretary of the R &WA.

It was an unforgettable experiene. God is Grace! One evening, Shri Jain came to my office when I was AD (Q). Shri Jain was virtually the Editor of the police magazine, The Indian Police Journal (IPJ), then brought out by the IB. Somehow, we liked each other. I was in the L Branch of the IB then, from where the IPJ used to be published. Shri G.C. Dutt, then DD (VIP) was officially the Editor of the IPJ. Shri G.C. Dutt was yet another giant of an officer, who had developed VIP security in India. More on him later.

Suddenly the question came out of me, "Well, Shri Jain, we find you coming to the office, go to the press and do everything for the IPJ even though your name figures nowhere in it. What exactly motivates you to do so". Shri Jain thought for a while and answered, "Sir, it is perhaps because I love the work". The answer acted like an electric shock to me. I jumped from my chair and went round and hugged for a while. He was a gentleman, passed his sixty. The lesson I learnt then stayed with me and I have been sharing it whenever I get an opportunity.

Shri A.K. Doval had been once the DIB and later on became the National Security Adviser (NSA) like MK. Currently, he is the most well-known IPS officer. He was AD, Aizwal when I was AD(Q), that is the desk officer for the NE. Ajit is one of the most dare devil officer after Shri M.K. Dhar. We corresponded via cipher on WT. He turned into Christian and started eating meat and drinking liquor. He could take any cover at a short notice. I had looked him at Aizawl. What a wonderful lady was his charming wife Anita! It was decided we should make out a case for awarding "Kirti Chakra", an army decoration. MK told me to give whatever we could and, he would do the rest. That he did. The citation for Ajit read that he used to roam about like a mendicant, etc. Truth was the casualty but the spirit that was there was correct. Ajit has been the only police officer to have received "Kirti Chakra".

It was decided to give out of turn Indian Police Medal to him. He is till today the youngest recipient of the IPM. Incidentally, I too got the IPM same year, superseding Shri D.C. Pathak, senior to me in the batch by one rank.

When Ajit was the Director at the Vivekananda International Foundation (VIF), he had the grace to publicly touch my feet and openly said that I was his "guru" in the IB. It was an over statement. But, look at the spirit and grace behind. It has indeed been a chela far outshining the guru.

Let me now go back in time to my highly privileged and affectionate relationship with Shri M.M.L. Hooja. I was like an advisor to him on Police matters when he was the DIB. I was then a voracious reader. As AD (L) I had read up all the Police Commission Reports, from the first 1902 Police Commission Report set-up by the Britishers. The first Police Commission Report in Independent India was set up in Bihar. It was written by no other than Shri K.N. Prasad. It has been in my humble opinion, the best Police Commission Report till the first All India Police Commission Report which was written by Shri C.V. Narasmahan, the first of the first of the 1948 batch of IPS officers. He was very articulate in projecting difficult matters. Clarity of thought was his forte. He had highly appreciated my response to the questionnaire by him. Going back to Shri Hooja, he had ensured that I went to the UNAFEI, "The United Nations Crime Prevention and Treatment of Offenders in Tokyo". I had missed out on that 3month long training course by a whisker the year before.

I learnt a lot at the UNAFEI, which was located at Fuchu, 30 miles from Tokyo. At the UNAFEI, except the Director, other members of the staff had to pay for telephone calls. I did the 31st International Course. As a trainee, I was asked to prepare a paper on the Indian Criminal Justice System. I had no papers with me. But, thanks to my district training under Shri Nirupam Som, I could make the note. It was appreciated and included in the UNAFEI publication. Our rooms used to be regularly dusted and cleaned in our absence by the families of the staff, including the wife of the Director.

The UNAFEI paid a lot of emphasis on treatment of offenders and the correctional system with emphasis on the system of probation.

The Japanese are known for their "Shistaachar". The majority of the Japanese work in private sector. When two such Japanese meet, they exchange visiting cards and then start bowing to each other. During this brief that time, they make assessment as to who among them was senior. Till the senior man would stop, the other man will continue bow. The height of the Japanese "shistaachar" is they cannot say no to anyone. They will say, "Yes, I do not agree with you".

The professors in Japan are highly valued and respected. The Japanese friends never asked questions. When asked about the reasons for that, they replied, "It is discourteous to ask questions to the seniors".

Foundational course was to end in December. We were out in the evening. It was bitter cold. When it was around 9 pm and there was not a single soul on the road. Traffic lights were on. Looking right and left, we tried to cross over. The Japanese friends held us back and firmly said, "No, No. You can't do it. It is red light. "We had to wait till the lights turned green.

The Japanese are a proud race. They get any book, however difficult or in whichever language, translated into Japanese language, within three days.

Before I leave Japan, it is time to get back to the manifestation of love and care on the part of Shri M.M.L. Hooja for his adviser on police matters D.C. Nath. He called me in Japan (Fuchu) and asked whether I would like to go on deputation to the MHA against a new post of Deputy Secretary just created. I was hesitating when Shri Hooja said, "You have just joined the IB.I think you should stay and build up your IB career". Later, there came an opportunity to go on deputation to the NPA. I had a knack for training assignment. Shri Hooja called me and said, "You are on deputation to the IB. There cannot be any better deputation than that ever".

Shri B.K. Mukherjee was my DD when I was AD (Q). He was what is called. God's good man. He was from Lahore. He could compose poems in Urdu. He joined the IB for the sake of his son's education. He had come from Tripura, where he was the State IGP. He tolerated all my antics. As AD (Q), I used to draft UO notes for him. This I would do mostly in the evening on our dinner table. At times, I would select words after carefully consulting the dictionary. In case, Shri Mukherjee would make any change, which was rightfully his privilege, I would go across to him and explain as to why I had used that expression. The UO notes those days were made on ultrathin rice paper. There were no computer then. If you have to make any change in the final UO note, you will have to very carefully rub off that portion, may be a word. It was a difficult job. By that standard, Shri Rattan Singh, my PA, mischievously called by his friends as "Rotton" Singh, had an easy job. He was rather fast in typing, He would just type out the draft that I would have written out in long hand the night before.

Shri Mukherjee always spoke about me in glowing terms. My friends used to pull my legs like this. "What "jadu" I had cast on him, that is what magic spell I had cast on him.

There was then the system of paying overtime those days. Shri Rattan Singh used to calculate the overtime from the time he had left home for the office till he would reach back home in the evening. His argument was simple. That period was not his.

Shri Mukherjee went back as the DGP of Madhya Pradesh, from where he superannuated. Whenever, he would come to Delhi, I would meet him. His son was doing studies in Delhi. He was good in studies.

After more than 10 years' stint at Hqrs, I was due to do some out station posting. I was posted to SIB Patna. But the DIB, Shri Mathur held back my release for reasons connected with operation.

Episode-16

Late B.N. Mullick once looked me up in Patna in the evening. He was then a sadhu. My wife enquired whether he would like tea or coffee. Shri Mullick said, "Ma, you would not know I eat only what I can cook. This is since my wife left me. I can take a glass of water from you if you have a steel glass. You yourself will re-wash the glass and give me a glass of water". We saw a real life saint! This was the man, before whom people, we are told, dared not to go.

Suddenly, my wife rang up and asked me to go to the residence. Shri K.P. Medhakar, who was my JD in IB Hqrs (He was the DJP in Maharashtra, from which post he had retired) was in my house. He asked,"Chitra! I am not feeling well. Could you please give me a glass of milk and two pieces of toasts? I have come to Patna in connection with the marriage of my elder brother's son. Instead of asking them for this, I thought I could come to you". Mr. Medhakar was extremely fond of me..

In Bihar, after my stay as the Deputy Director there for about six months, I was told to prepare a report on the problems in the State. I went round, met as many senior officers, politicians and many others in all walks of life as I could. The report was highly appreciated, as told to me by Shri R.K. Khandelwal. This study stood me in great stead in Bihar.

Shri Khandelwal came to Patna. Patna was my first out station. I experimented with a lot of my ideas. I had introduced the maintenance of the history of the post so that the new incumbent could start his innings with some background knowledge and confidence. Over the years, the history of the post would be of great help. Shri Khandelwal told me to send a suitable note on the subject to the Training Centre in IB Hqrs for recommending that on all India basis. He observed,"Dhanesh, I have a lot to learn from you".

There was a DCIO in Patna, Shri S.N. Singh, known as Sachidababu. What a team man he was! He would write out reports for/on behalf of juniors so that they get the credit to get promotion.

I was at Patna for six years. We occasionally organised annual picnics. The turn-out in the first ever such picnic was over 500. This included ladies also. The next year, the ladies started enquiring from my wife when would be the next picnic. With officers like Sachidababu and RNP Singh, an outstanding operation man, you could do anything you wanted.

It so happened Shri T.V. Rajeshwar's first outstation visit as the DIB was Patna. There was a bad case of Harijan burning. We had the information about that and had advised the Bihar govt on that in writing. Shri Rajeshwar flew to Patna taking with the Union Home Minister. In the meeting with the State officials, we were on top. Soon after, Shri Rajeshwar again came to Patna. It appeared to me that he came for relaxation. There was no inspection, no visit to the SIB office. We went round the city, went to the newly constructed road bridge across the Ganges to Hajipur. I took him to the Chief Secretary Shri Ramasubramanian. He told Shri Rajeshwar, "Nath is so close to us that we believe he is our officer". It had been so decent to me indeed!

We were on top on intelligence in both Patna and at AD Jamshedpur with Nehchal Sandhu who later became DIB. In the first, and the last also, CIO's conference at IB Hqrs, the Hqrs. Deputy Director complained of some deficiency in the coverage in some areas in the present Jharkhand area. Before my CIO could say anything, I stood up and strongly protested,

"We know every inch of the area like the palm of my hand. Please specify where we have failed". MK intervened "Leave that. I want to catch Dhanesh somewhere else."

When on transfer, I was going to Calcutta, almost all Hqrs staff were at the railway station to bid me good bye. I was in tears and so were many among the staff. I also cried and said, I would come again. I did go to Patna again, when I was JD, SIB, Calcutta.

We were on a operation that took us to Calcutta. We obtained the services of one technical officer from the IB Hqrs Shri S.K. Gupta. He was a man of very high integrity, a hallmark of the officers, of the IB officers in general. We would always get equipment from western countries tested for applicability under our typical tropical conditions. We would not accept any equipment unless certified by SK. We had a report that Indian agents of a foreign country had made an abortive attempt on SK.

Once on an operation in hand, it was both very delicate and difficult. Nehchal and I were in Calcutta. At a particular point of time, SK got stuck up at a place and in a manner, where if he were to stay for long he would have been churned to death. SK suffered but did not flinch. He had overcome the normal human instinct of survival.

While in Delhi, we would send SK for all delicate operations. I am proud of someone like SK to work with. On his retirement, SK started his own company. While at the IISSM on which we would speak later, I had sought for his services when necessary. Our relationship remained very sweet..

This is yet another case of experimenting my idea in SIB, Patna. An ACIOI joined Patna. I learnt he was highly disgruntled. I sent for him. He explained how he had been wronged for no fault of his. His ACR had been spoilt and his juniors had gone up the ladder. Somehow, I believed his account. I had learnt that he could write well. I posted him at Muzzafarpur, an important posting. We had a deal. He would do this much, I would do three times more for him. He abided by the agreement. I started giving him good, better to best ACRs. By God's grace, he got his promotion. This gave me great satisfaction.

Experiments after experiments we had started the annual best source report writing competition. The officers would be called in batches of three/four at a time. I would check the reports and tried to make improvement where required. One report by ACIOI, Samastipur won the best source report in the first year. I felt that to be the model source report. I sent that to the Hqrs Training School. The ıdea was appreciated.

We had a highly dedicated team for preparing the data for sending post election review report. The team had worked for four days and nights at the office for preparing the required data. There were no computers then. So, one had to do all the hard work manually. Shri D.N. Singh, ACIO-I, was in-charge of the election cell. DN had given me all the details I had asked for. I sat down to dictate the report but to my horror, I realised that I had failed to ask for some data without which I could not start the dictation. And, I did not have the heart to tell the election cell to attempt prepare the data when the members of the election were all set to go home after 4 days & nights in the office. Sharing my thoughts with Mohan, my PA, an excellent Keralite youngman, I was brooding over the matter with my head down, Mohan disappeared and told DN. Suddenly, DN appeared before me and asked as to what had happened. I explained. Without battling an eye lid, he said, "Sir, please do not worry, *Ghar jaiye*. We are not going home tonight. *Kal subah apko details mil jayega, do baje flight me apka report chala jayega"*.

I have no words to express my feelings at that time. It is a matter of great pride to work with staff like D.N. Singh.

Once, the then DIB Shri Rajeshwar called up to say that he would be reaching Patna in another about two hours' time or so with the then Prime Minister, "Please go and inform the Chief Secretary for the needful. The Chief Secretary was having a meeting. I barged in, went near him and conveyed the message. He drove out the officers. The Prime Minister,

Smt. Indira Gandhi came. Shri Rajiv Gandhi was the pilot. He preferred to sit in the plane for all the time.

DGP, Bihar, was then Shri S.K. Chatterjee. In a meeting in Chief Secretary's room, he once asked me "Well, Mr. Nath, you have only 4-5 members of staff, as against we having at least 10 and more in each district. How do you get information so quickly? It came out of my mouth instinctively. I replied "Sir, it is perhaps because of the culture of the organisation". We were on the top.

I enjoyed my meetings with the State Governor Dr. A.R. Kidwai, a scion of the Kidwai family. He was a Botanist by profession and choice. The Raj Bhawan garden was then something to see. He had sent a letter to the Union Home Minister, recommending, Prime Minister's Medal for me. MK had not got that till then. Had that somehow materialised, that would have been a catastrophe.

Whenever I visited Patna from Delhi, Dr. Kidwai insisted on my staying at the Raj Bhawan The best evidence of my love with Dr. Kidwai was that I had my parting dinner in Patna at the Raj Bhawan.

The Chief Secretary Shri O.P. Nayyar was a work horse. There was an eight-seater plane, its pilot for ages was Capt. A K Singh. He could fly the plane in any inclement weather. Any incident anywhere, a team comprising the Chief Minister, the Chief Secretary, IG, State Intelligence Branch and myself would fly down to the nearest airfield, stay there for an hour or two and would then fly back. This practice proved very effective. Other State officers started saying that Shri Nayyar had come under my influence. Inside the plane the cassette on *Hanuman Chalisa* was always on.

We had gone, by an eight-seater plane to Jamshedpur and came back to Ranchi. At both the places, the Chief Minister Jagannath Mishra gave the assurance that the Police Commissionorate system would soon be introduced at both the places.

On return to Patna, I was talking to the Chief Secretary Shri O.P. Nayyar in his favour. He told me, "DC, do you think the Police Commissionarate system could be introduced unless I, as the Chief Secretary, agree?" I was stunned. He had not said a single word on this in the plane on our way back.

We had the same experience in Delhi. Shri T.N. Chaturvedi was the IGP, Delhi. In the annual IGP conference, the incumbent Union Home Minister said, "I am all for it." Pointing both hands at the Union Home Secretary, he further added *"In log hone denge, tab to, kam boney"*.

Well, this is harsh reality. The political leaders do not rule the country. The IAS fraternity does.

I had a fantastic team in Patna, comprising S/Shri S.N. Singh, R.N.P. Singh et al. We could take on any task. MK once told the flag of SIB Patna flew at the highest. It was a great feeling.

Shri S.N. Mishra, who had joined as the section officer gave me a sound advice. We have annual picnics. Shri Mishra said that we could treat those picnics as convening general body meetings, for which Rs 1.50 per head were allowed. That would reduce the burden on other resources. There was no hanky panky or dishonesty involved. We can always learn.

At Patna, I had peculiar relationship with the then Chief Minister Dr. Jagannath Mishra. This was relating the appointment of judges to the High Court. A certificate of financial integrity of the candidates from the MHA (read-IB) was a must then. The system was that the Chief Justice would recommend. That would require the concurrence of the Chief Minister and the State Governor. Dr. Mishra was interested in 4 candidates, We did agree on two of his candidates. He was furious and complained to the Union Home Minister. He knew about our objection. The Union Home Minister flew down to Patna. Dr. Kidwai had already briefed me. We got the matter rechecked. I was called, I stood our ground. The Prime Minister Smt. Gandhi went by our report. Dr. Mishra met the

Prime Minister without any success. He, however, got them through soon after Smt. Gandhi.

Socio-cultural activities in Patna were very regular, at least once in two months. I followed the principle of the first to arrive at the scene and the last to go. Bhojpuri songs and humours won the day. One song in demand was "**Khaike Panwala**" in the lips of Amitabh.

We had annual picnics. The Bihari ladies are generally 'pardanasin' but they are smart indeed! In the first year's picnic, the turn out of the ladies were not more than 100. Having heard how good was the picnic, their number went upto about 150. Thereafter, they started enquiring from my wife as to the date of the next picnic.

In the socio-cultural functions, we wanted every lady to join. If nothing else, nobody could say she did not know how to play the game of baggadoli. You have just to throw up the round balls with the stick. Then, nobody could deny she did not to play the game of Dart. You aim your dart at the board in front of you and throw. The idea was everyone should get a prize. It was, something like a non-winners' prize would be given to every participant. I remember we had given a handkerchief to each of the participants.

It was not all work and no play. We all would be out of the office between 4 pm and 6 pm. We played volleyball, table tennis and badminton. And, be back to work we had introduced "Nath Challenge Shield" for all round competence from an individual. After I had left Patna, it was still in use. I offered to get the Shield polished and that was done. ACIOII R.R. Sahay won the Shield for the first year and he continued to get it for several years. I had forgotten to mention the names of two members of the team of Sachidababu, both ACIOI. One was Ambica Sahay and the other was Nareshbabu.

We were having lunch at the lawn of my house. MK, the incumbent DIB, was in Patna along with Rattan Sehgal. Nareshbabu was so professional in looking after the guests that when towards the end, Nareshbabu came forward and introduced himself, DIB said, "I thought you are the head of caterers". We had a hearty laugh and Nareshbabu found out what he could do after retirement!

In volleyball, ACIO I (WT) Bhalla and self were always on opposite sides. Bhalla smashed very hard. I often succeeded in blocking his hard smashes. Jagdish would be jumping in joy.

Bhalla was, however, unstoppable in badminton. Monomaybabu was good but was no match for Bhalla.

It would not be inappropriate to delve in some aspects of Bihar's societal habits. I have toured Bihar extensively and I know Bihar better than West Bengal. It was told that I was one-fifth Bihari. You have not known Bihar or Biharis unless you have seen Bihari villagers immersed in singing loudly, uttering only "**Rama Ho**" nonstop for two hours or so, even after the day's hard labour. There is some magic in it. This two hours' non-stop chanting of "**Rama Ho**" leads them to sound sleep and would rejuvenate them for the next day's work afresh. What a simple living style, that goes unknown and unsung to the countrymen! Oh, Men!, know thy country. We bet you cannot beat a Bihari in chanting *Hanuman Chalisa*. One can say I had my religious indoctrination in Patna.

I have been in love with the SIB, Patna. I have been in love with Bihar as well to earn that sobriquet that I am one-fifth Bihari.

I have spent a large part of the book on what all I did or experimented upon on my ideas while at my first field posting to SIB, Patna. This had everything of intelligence problems that the IB Hqrs had. So, briefed me my benefactor and well-wisher Shri S.N. Mathur, the then DIB.

We did our best to work out plans accordingly.

This is what had happened in a quarterly conference, Shri S.N. Singh was then DCIO. He was like my brother and comrade in arms. By way of encouraging officer to raise sources in difficult areas, money was a handicap. MK had sent us some money. We distributed that money among the DCIOs, adding they were free to spend that money in any manner they liked. They would not be held accountable to explain how did they spend that money. It was added that if necessary, more money would be given to them for this work.

We took stock of the matter in two successive quarterly meetings. No positive result was reported. At the next quarterly conference, Sachidababu (Shri S.N. Singh) said, "Sir, we have not been able to spend the money at all. Our middle class mentality did not permit us to spend money when we were not certain about the result". I was stunned. This brought in bold relief the stark honesty of the officers. They returned the money on the spot. What a privilege to lead such a team!

It was 2nd January. We had selected a kind of an island on the bed of the Ganges. It was bitter cold. Yet, the turn-out was very good. The estimated food fell short. About 15 of us had our food from a dhaba on the river bank. We paid for our food individually. Nobody had grumbled. That was the team spirit we had been able to build up. It was indeed a happy moment. The team spirit on display made me feel happy.

No wonder that MK had said that the flag of SIB Patna then flew the highest.

Despite my tiff with Dr. Mishra, it will be interesting to know, we had a good rapport on many issues and I enjoyed his confidence. More on that slightly later.

I was sitting in my office. Suddenly, a gentleman turned up. He has just been selected as a Judge in Patna High Court. He knew the process of selection of Judges and the importance of the role of the SIB in it. He said, "Mr. Nath, I came to thank you and also to say good bye. After assuming charge, the judges become totally unsocial. And, so, there may not be any occasion for us to meet again." We enjoyed a cup of tea. Well, we have still men like him. An ideal gentleman to meet. I cherish that occasion even now.

Dr. Mishra would usually call me up around 11 pm to cross check with us the information received by him from the State Intelligence Branch. Shri D.N. Sahay, my batchmate, was then the DIG, State IB. He later on became the Governor, Tripura. He was an ideal intelligence officer. He would have been an asset for the IB.I had the occasion to stay with him at Agartala Raj Bhawn years later. Thanks to him. I had the benefit of darshan of Tripureshwar and Kamleshar. That was a privilege. Thank you D.N.

Shri N.N. Singh (RR), known as the NN Junior because there was a senior N N Singh also. He was an excellent friend. We played a lot of bridge together. He had gone on deputation to the CBI for some years. He stayed there and had become the Additional Director/Special Director. An anecdote for diversion. We were playing bridge at NN's house. When snacks came, NN avoided the non-vegetarian snacks. When I asked that some of them were enjoying drinks, what was the problem with the non-vegetarian snacks for him. N N came out with a stunning answer. "Dhanesh, this is pure vegetarian food". We had a hearty laugh. It was indeed a privilege to know such an officer.

Shri B.R. Lal was the IGP when I had joined SIB Patna. I called on him duly. He was very stiff and answered in term of "Yes" or "No". In the next room was DN. I told him about this. He explained that Shri Lal had a tiff with my predecessor and hence he might have behaved like that.

Shri Lal had an old Chevrolet car. A time came Shri Lal planned his long distance journey by road in a manner that I could travel with him. He used to sit cross legged on the seat. That posture, he explained, made you feel less tired and was good for your back. In any case, I scored a victory on him and felt happy.

After Dr. Mishra, the new Chief Minister was Shri Bhagawat Jha Azad, DN introduced me to him. After preliminaries, I placed my services to him and told him, "Sir, one thing you will have to avoid was the *'sab thik hai'* culture of his predecessor". I explained Dr. Mishra had the style, when meeting the people, of raising both his hands and do say, *sab thik hai*? That evoked prompt response, *"ji huzur, sab thik hai"*. Dr. Mishra was careful that the pressmen were around. We had a hearty laugh. The ice was broken. Thanks to Shri D.N. Sahay.

I had gone to Bhagalpur in connection with the infamous Bhagalpur blinding case. Jagdishbabu, the DCIO, was helpful. Vishnu Dayal was the SP. Vishnu is now an elected MP.

On another occasion, Jagdishbabu took me to Mungher. We went to the house where Rabindranath Thakur has spent some time.

After the work was over, I was waiting for the state plane to pick me up. We received a disconcerting news that the plane might not come. Jagdish, my driver, said, *"Koi bat nei. Hum by road se hi chalenge"*. I had some urgency to come early so as to prepare a report that had to catch the afternoon flight to Delhi. Jagdish made the two hours' distance in one-and-a-half hour' time. I was sitting with eyes closed and drafting the report in mind.

Jagdish deserves a few words on him. He was from UP. He was proud of driving me all the time. The second driver, Akhilesh, hardly got any chance. Jagdish loved the black ambassador car. Every morning, Jagdish in his *"langoti"* washed the car religiously.

Jagdish was honest and helpful to all. One night, he woke me up at around 2am.Some lady was to be taken to the hospital. Officers were debating how to wake me up to get my permission to use the car. Jagdish came forward and took my permission.

Jagdish loved me. My sons were very fond of him. On retirement, Jagdish went back to his village in Moradabad. One morning he suddenly met me in Delhi. He brought some homemade food stuff. He did not want any favour. Jagdish with his moustache was the same person with hairs turning somewhat grey.

An anecdote worth sharing. My elder son was in the market. He had grown beards and was chubby. The shop owner took him to be a Sardar boy in his effort to sell his product, he said, *"Sardarji log wohi pasand karta hai"*.

On return home, Debashis told us about this. We had a hearty laugh.

In Patna, we had by and large worked out the routine that all of us were out of the office at 4pm. Some played volleyball, some played badminton and some played table tennis. We would be back to work at 6 pm.

Shri Dwivedi was the assistant technical officer. Once the dyanamo had gone out of order. Dwivedi went under the machine and would not come out for food or attending to the call of nature. He was determined to come out only after setting the machine right. He did exactly that. He came out with a smile of victory writ large on his face. We all felt happy. Dwivedi has two bright sons.

We had a grand reception on arrival at Patna. Shri S.N. Singh, (the senior) was at the airport. He took us straight to the *Hanuman Mandir* in the heart of the market near the railway station. From there we reached 6, Surpentine Road, which was the official residence for the DD, SIB, Patna. When DIB Shri Mathur posted me to Patna, he said, "Well Chatterjee (My nick name in that 'operation'), you have a house which is better than my house at 9, Tughlaq Road. This house has three bed rooms of similar type on the eastern side and the western side. During the winter you can stay on eastern wing and during the summer you can shift the western wing.

Shri Mathur had also said you have, everything of intelligence in Bihar that we have in the IB. Shri Mathur had apparently forgotten to mention that the house at 6 Surpentine Road was based on 6 acres of land with staff quarters for everyone. The house had a number of plants of banana, guava, blackberry, mango, amla and what not.

There was also a diminutive sized window, who would run up and pick up the clothes at the sight of clouds gathering and raindrops dropping. You do not have to bother. There were two maalis – one is to look after the gardening and the other, a former army jawan, would help him.

On arrival at house, senior S.N. Singh, *"Sir aapka khana*

mera ghar". We did not understand the meaning, Sachidababu explained. When we came back after the lunch, we received a trunk call (there were no cell phone those days), from the elder son of my wife's elder sister, *"Moshiji kya haal chaal chho*?" My wife handed over the phone to me.

There was a special sweet, called "SWARBHAJA" in Aarrah district. It has a hard crust. When you bite it, sweet juice would come out and could spoil your dress. Only two families prepared this sweet at least for long. There was then sour *dahi* from Habra. It was so stiff that nothing will fall down even if you hold the earthen pot upside down.

You have not known Bihar if you have not tasted "litty" that is put in some kind of a ditch and then charcol fire is put over that place. The litty would be ready after about one hour. If you are a non-Bihari, we bet one litty is enough as a meal. You need to drink a lot of water to facilitate its digestion. And, if you do not have strong teeth, never try a litty.

Chhat is the biggest Hindu festival in North Bihar. A large number of Biharis go on leave to join this festival. This is *Surya Pronam*. You should be at the riverside near Patna Medical College. it is an early morning event. Gracious ladies will float the 'diyas' and dump bananas into the river. Youngsters are there in the water to grab those bananas.

These days, Chhat festival is also observed in metropolitan cities like Delhi and Bombay. At around 6 'o'clock in the morning you can hear gun shot.

"Thekua" is an essential part of chhatparab. It is a home-made sweet, We even now get annual supply of this home-made sweet.

S.N. Singh, the senior, knew almost all those one needed to know as an intelligence officer. You leave him with his PA, who had seven daughters. S.N. Singh would just tell the facts to his PA, the report will be done.

We had the typical Darbhanga Dahi-chura in the house of Shri Awadh Kumar Jha,who was a journalist.

We were at Ranchi. My wife's eldest sister was patting our son to sleep, putting on her shoulder. "Yes, Sir, Yes Sir, three bags full". My son, protested, "No, my father is D C Nath."

Shri Singh had introduced me to a Minister Shri Vidyakar Kavi. He was a staunch Hindu. Among his daily morning's schedule was reading aloud the religious scripture, namely, *Durgasaptsati*. He had been doing so for years. One fine morning, he stopped doing so on the ground it was no point reading the *Durgasaptsati* when the mind was away. There is an important lesson to learn from Vidyakar Kavi. We wish we had more Vidyakar Kavi ji.

Gaya is known for 'pindadan'. There is an area in the outskrits of Gaya, where if you are within an area of a mile or so, you will enjoy the fragrance of something being fried in *suddha ghee* from cow milk. That is 'anarsa'.

There is a temple in Gaya, called Vishnu Mandir. There is a foot-print one inch in-depth inside the temple. It is almost unbelievable.

Jhumritilaya is mid-way between Patna and Ranchi. We stopped there for a cup of tea. Jagdish told the stall-owner to make special for his boss. When the tea came, it was a concussion of milk, tejpata, addrak, tulsipata and sugar. We went to the stall-owner and told him to put fresh water in the kettle. He had no tea leaves. He had tea dust. He had only dudh tea. We said that we would put the quantity of dust tea and shall add to our test. We then proceeded.

We have occasionally stayed at the guest rooms on the banks of Jhumritilaya barrage. It commands a grand view.

Episode-17

I was in SIB Calcutta. One evening around 10 pm, Shri Barari, then DIB, called up and said, "Dhanesh, there has been some communal riot in Murshidabad (a district in West Bengal). You may not have got any information. Do ring up the DCIO and let me hear back". We did so and passed on the information to Shri Barari. That was leadership. It made me feel happy.

A Minister of State in Delhi was on a visit to Calcutta. We never knew about it. He called me up around 5pm. and disclosing his identity, he took me to task, stating, "Do you know I am your Minister? I was attacked in Behala. You never told me." We had heard over radio news around 2 pm about him being so appointed. I told him, "Sir, we have heard about your appointment but we had no information of the incident that you told me. In any case, even if we had the information, I would have sent that to the IB Hqrs only and not to you". That infuriated him. He asked me to see him in the evening at 7 pm at the hotel where he was staying. I once again explained to him. He asked me to take down some message he wanted to send to the Union Home Secretary that I should send over teleprinter. I did so with a copy to MK. I also rang him up and told him the entire story.

On his return to Delhi, the Minister took charge and went to call on the Prime Minister Smt Indira Gandhi as the Minister of State, Home Affairs. The PM sent for the Union Home Secretary and the DIB (MK). She gave a dressing down to the

Minister and told him to read the rules of procedure first. She firmly told the Minister that the Joint Director was absolutely right. I felt vindicated and happy.

It must, however, be said in favour of the Minister that he admitted this in a some closed door meeting soon thereafter where I was present. No body other than me and the DIB knew anything about all this.

Debu (D. Bandopadhyay from the IB Hqrs). was asking Naparajit (Naparajit Mukherjee, who later became the DGP, West Bengal), my AD to give an assessment of trends in the election. Naparajit came to me. I told him to inform Debu that we could not give the trend, which is actually not possible. Debu might have enquired from Naparajit several times during the course of the day. I told him to repeat that we could not give the trend. Towards the evening, Naparajit came almost in tears and said, "Sir, Debuda tells me that they have got the trend from all other SIB' and he will now tell MK about us." MK, we learnt, told Debu, "Well, if Dhanesh has said so, do not press him. He will never give it". MK knew all that was fuss. One thing about the election. Never tell the ruling party that they were going to loose. If they really win, you can take the credit we told you so. In case they loose, who bothers about them when they were not in power and were gone!

I was then the Special Director. Here, is an interesting anecdote. I had gone from Delhi in connection with election review. The district officers were giving their appreciation. Amiya Samanta who was the Joint Director in SIB Calcutta, holds the record of having done most districts, frequently interrupted the field officers, by way of poohpohing them, and thereby exposing their what he felt inadequacies. Possibly, Amiya failed to take notice of the fact that the time had changed. It soon appeared that the field officers started feeling uncomfortable. Those who were yet to speak kept themselves a little reserved.

Tushar, who was the DD, SIB, Calcutta, suddenly intervened and almost non-challantly told Amiya, "Sir, at

times, it is good not to know so much. Kindly, let the district officers tell us what is their present day assessment".

When I had joined as DD, SIB, Calcutta, there was an AD(E), Shri A N Bose, a very trustworthy officer. When on the first day, he came to me, I told him he could leave the files with me. I would see these duly. With no reflections on senior predecessors, he got the message and said, *"Are dekhi files dekhte chai"*, meaning thereby that this DD wanted to see files.

I had learnt from Shri S.K. Mishra who was my SO(E) for sometime in SIB Patna the importance of the establishment work. Many senior officers neglect this work at great cost to the organisation. Shri Mishra had risen to the rank of the Joint Director. He is the only ministerial hand to have achieved that. He had joined as an assistant, unlike Shri Venkatachari, who had started as the LDC.

Shri Misha gave a sound advice. We used to have annual picnics. He said that we could treat those picnics as convening general body meetings, for which Re1.50 per head were allowed. That would reduce the burden on other resources. There was no hanky panky or dishonesty involved. We can always learn.

As in SIB Patna, we had formidable team in SIB, Calcutta also. Here, the team comprised IPS officers. They were: S/Shri T.K. Mitra (Tushar), S.K. Banerjee (Sujit) in Calcutta and Tapan Chattopadhyay at Siliguri. Tushar looked after internal intelligence and Sujit was in charge of counter intelligence.

The beauty in CI work lies in the fact that at times,one comes in possession of very uncomfortable information about one's friends. Friendship may lead you to feel inclined to warn off friends to stay away but professionalism would not permit that. We faced an extremely embarrassing case when Shri Vaidya was the DIB. We had received a report. Shri Vaidya told me, "Dhanesh, destroy the paper. Now, only you and me know of .this. "I must compliment the field unit that had sent up the report.

Shri S.P. Talukdar was DD(E) in IB Hqrs. The Establishment Branch had transferred out one Shri Bardhan on the ground of his long stay in Calcutta. I had written a d.o. letter to Satyen to cancel the order on the ground of the need to retain him in Calcutta. I had ended up the letter that he could transfer me out, because, "DDs may come and go, but Bardhan must stay in SIB for the sake of smooth working of the SIB". Satyen must have enjoyed that. He called me up. We had a friendly chat for long. Shri Bardhan was retained in Calcutta, I felt happy.

At times, my relationship with MK turned sour. In a conference at the IB Hqrs, MK was determined to target the operation group in the counter intelligence group. He was after MK Rathindran. When Rathindran failed to satisfy him, he turned to me and enquired what I had to say. I was ready both mentally and with facts and figures. I told MK, "Sir, you have seen our report. With the given/depleted staff, nothing more can be done." It then came out of me, "Sir, if you wish, you can wind up the entire CI Group. MK realised the seriousness of my complaint. In a way, he was caught in his own trap. Addressing Shri Vaidya, MK said,"Vaidya, see, see, what Dhanesh is saying". Right at that time, the peon came in and said that there was an important and urgent call for MK on the RAX. Shri Vaidya told us to break for coffee. All those present at the conference jumped om me, accusing me, it was highly improper on my part to have told DIB to wind up the CI group.

I was in Calcutta. MK was the Governor of the State. From the office of the JD, Calcutta, I got in touch with the Secretary to the Governor, telling him to leave a message to his boss that I was in town for a few days. Pat came the reply, asking to join MK at lunch.

I had a hearty lunch. MK first asked me what prompted me to leave a message that I was in town. Amu, by which name we used to address Smt Narayanan, had prepared non-vegetarian food for me. It was rasogulla at the end.

Prof. Nurul Hassan was at the Raj Bhawan when I was the DD, SIB, Calcutta. Prof Hassan was an erudite scholar. Even in those days, he talked about the silk road. He was very fond of me. I used to spend a lot of time with him. Prof Hassan was a very fat man, yet he liked his food. I benefited much sitting with him. My fortnightly d.o. letters to the DIB, were referred to by MK as models.

MK (then DIB), had in his wisdom, appointed me as the Inspector General for the IB. I felt proud. It gave me an opportunity to know many things that would not have been known to many including DIBs. The establishment group in the Hqrs. became both scared and unhappy with me. This assignment also gave me the opportunity to discover many talents in different SIBs. There was an assistant Bhaskar who had on his own initiative learnt the computers. The process of introduction of computers in the IB was still going on.

The concerned assistant was then under order of transfer to the N-E.I was able to get that change and got him to the IB Hqrs and got him posted to the computer cell. I felt I had done a good job.

A word on Shri P. (Prabir) K. Mullick, then DD, SIB, Calcutta. A thorough gentleman, he was a thorough professional too. Even as an Assistant Director, he had taken on the redoubtable and a terror to many, Shri B.N. Mullick, was the DIB then. While on an operation, he was in the field, Shri Mullick wanted Prabirda to do a certain thing in a particular manner. This was in cipher on WT. Prabirda replied, "Sir, I am in the field. This cannot be done, Shri Mullick got stumped but could not do anything. What you have said cannot be done. I am doing it in this manner". The terror DIB had to accept that.

Prabirda had an excellent handwriting. He was a straight forward officer. He did not bend down to certain request made to the DIB Shri Atma Jayram by one of his friends. Prabirda had to suffer for that.

He was so helpful to me when I happened to be staying in Calcutta in connection with an operation. I used a lot of money then. Prabirda was meticulous in making arrangements for 21"rebels" we had gathered in Calcutta, They were there for about 10 days and then flew back. The Calcutta police did not know anything about it. Prabirda was a model to the younger service colleagues. I had learnt a lot from him.

I had drawn up a detailed welfare scheme for the staff. At the quarterly conference, the post incharge was required to bring the list of grievances of each member of the staff posted at the unit. The grievances should be in two parts. First, the grievances, in respect of which, action lay with the IB Hqrs. The SIB will forward that or those to the IB, with previous references, if any. Before coming to the quarterly conferences, every post incharge was supposed to have enquired from each member of the staff if they had any personal problems or difficulties, in which we from the SIB Hqrs could help. These could relate children's admission to school, requirement of financial help for medical reasons, marriage of daughters, et al.

As I had learnt while at Patna, I would take up establishment work first. Thus, sitting in my office, we could monitor that things were under control. This was a kind of close partnership business that worked well.

I was fond of talking to the officer and men, especially on occasions like the Republic Day or the Independence Day. In the course of my talk on one such occasion, I somehow came upon the subject of motivation, normally taught in IIMs. One theory of motivation is X-Y. Red eyes versus a pat at the back. I always believed a pat on the back was better of the two. I further developed it to say that "You love yourself the most". I continued, "You, therefore, try to put up your best face to your boss, to your friends as also before the members of your family. So, the self-motivation was the best form of motivation." I continued, "So, friends, Love Thyself".

I heard officers leaving the place, murmuring," Love Thyself. This was a moment of great happiness to me.

In SIB, Calcutta, I once utilised a part of Japanese management technology. At a quarterly conference, I asked the participants to give me in one and half page and in three parts on: "What do you think of the (a) Tasks before your unit; (b) Tasks before the SIB, and (c) Tasks before the IB Hqrs in five years hence. Some officers enquired how could they think of the IB Hqrs. No explanation was given. They were told to THINK, THINK, THINK and THIINK. They did. I compiled their thoughts and sent that to IB Hqrs. It was highly appreciated.

In between, I had overheard some of the officers saying, "It was for the first time that a senior officer had asked us to THINK for the organisation. I felt very happy.

Some of us students of the Calcutta Presidency College and a few others went for picnics. We had gone to the Sundarbans and spent a full moon night on the launch(small steamer). The journey through the "khairis" with the fear of a Royal Bengali tiger jumping on us always at the back of our mind, was enjoyable.

We also had occasional singing sessions at each other's house. A class friend Dr. Asim Roy, now based at southernmost island of Ausrtalia, namely, Hobart, looked forward to these evenings. One of our nieces, Tapu is a notable singer of Rabindra sangeet. We at times invited her to join us. She kept us enthralled.

We occasionally joined steamer parties organised by the alumni of Calcutta Presidency College Branch of the Alumni Association. Those were unforgettable occasions.

Subimal, a junior officer, was an MA in Bengali and was an excellent singer. His composition of scripts was superb. Shri BB Kar had by then taken over from Shri Bose. His elder daughter was good in Nazrul songs. Subimal drafted her suitably.

Ashok's younger daughter Kamalini is a proponent of Rabindra sangeet. She has sung 40 songs in the famous cassette containing 1000 Rabindra sangeets.

We at times held the musical programmes outside also. My wife joined in singing and I recited poems.

Shri P.K. Mukherjee once brought some friends from outside and had a two hour long 'shruti natak' on Jajabar's famous book "Drishtipat". It was really a professional programme.

Once, we were returning from the Andamans after attending the annual Police Science Congress. On landing at Calcutta Airport, seniors asked Shri Medhakar, who was then DGP, Mahrashtra to join for lunch. Inside the plane, I was sitting by the side of Shri Medhakar. He was an expert in writing limmericks. He wrote a number of those effortlessly. I had told Shri Medhakar that my wife Chitra would cook hilsha fish for him.

Shri Medhakar stunned all. "I will have my lunch with Dhanesh but will like to see you in office before leaving for the airport in the evening. He had his lunch with me.

In IB Hqrs, I had a tiff with Shri Medhakar on a typical issue.I had written the ACR on my Section Officer (of the Q Branch) Shri Venkatachari and sent up to Shri Medhakar. Mr B.K. Mukherjee was yet to join as my Deputy Director. Shri Medhakar returned the ACR stating that I had written it in rather superlative terms. I sent back the ACR, writing "Sir, I have written what I had thought best. I would be grateful, if it pointed out where l had used superlative terms". That. ACR never came to me. Let me add I was not an obdurate officer. What happened is I had just sent up the ACR Shri Venkatachari had written on one of his assistance Rajinder Kumar. It was indeed in glowing terms. Having seen that, I decided that I, in my turn, would write the ACR on Shri Venkatachari better than what he had written on Rajinder.

It so happened that Shri Arun Mukherjee, who had been my SP in Darjeeling, Shri T.A. Chari and Sankarda, my batch mate in service, were posted in Calcutta when I was DD, SIB, Calcutta, We hit upon an idea to organise a two daylong Seminar in Calcutta. The subject related to an in-depth analysis of police issue. Nothing of this type had taken place before. In that sense, this made history. Dr. Arun Mukherjee presided.

We had gathered some eminent social scientists from different parts of the country. The venue was the IIM, just in the outskirts of Calcutta. Shri Chari had played a special role in raising the vital financial resources. Smt Chari, who was a lawyer by profession, had helped in this matter.

The event went as per schedule and was a thumping success. In the process, I too became a part of history.

In addition to picnics and other enjoyable socio-cultural activities, we would once a quarter visit our sister in the outskirts of Calcutta for a couple of days. All the sons and members of their families gathered. We had hell of a time .We returned rejuvenated and happy.

At SIB, Calcutta, I once organised an inter SIB games. Necessary permission was obtained from Shri R.K. Kapoor, then DIB. Officers and staff came from SIB, Bhubaneshwar, Siliguri, Gangtok, The games were held at SIB Kalimpong. This generated considerable enthusiasm among all. This was the first and last such games.

I had introduced/ donated "Best Athlete Challenge Shield" first at SIB, Patna, when I was DD there. It is a running shield. It was then introduced in SIB, Calcutta also. The Shield at SIB, Patna was still there when I had last inquired.

I was fond of holding quarterly conferences. There was no big room in SIB, Calcutta to hold such conferences. I got a 20 ft by 40 ft oval shaped structure raised. The Commissioner of Police, Calcutta and State Chief Secretary had joined us. It was a matter of great satisfaction.

In the first meeting of the SIB recreation club, SIB, Calcutta, about 12/13 members were present out of about 30 members. I issued instructions that if the DD/Joint Director of the SIB could attend, all others could also do please. In other words, attendance at the meetings of the recreation club was made compulsory. We had a welfare officer also in this recreation club. One Shri Sankar Das, an LDC then, was given the responsibility and Sankar did discharge that responsibility with extreme sincerity. I happened to be in touch with Sankar even today.

As I had introduced annual picnics in SIB Patna, I started the same thing in Calcutta. We took WT sets in order to keep in touch with, if the need be, with the office. The wives of DCIOs told me that they had never before been to the premises of the SIB before.

It had by then become a veteran for annual Police Science Congress. It was at Bangalore. My paper was on ***Tasks Before the Indian Police in 2005***". It was a futuristic projection before the 21st century started.

Shri V.S. Saigal, the then Special Director was a journalist before joining the service. He wrote well. We were to prepare for Shri Rajiv Gandhi his maiden speech at the DGP Conference. I was called by MK. It was decided we should give some forward-looking material to the Prime Minister .It was a proud moment for me.

My batch mate Shri J.N. Roy covered some very sensitive desk. From discussions with him, I was convinced that had the Government in the centre listened to 40 percent of the information the IB had conveyed, many big catastrophes could have been avoided.

For purpose of change, here is an interesting anecdote. A friend of mine elder to me by two years, had gone for an interview. A common question those days related to hobbies. Being a brilliant student of literature, he had prepared a rather intelligent answer. He somehow managed to manoeuvre the board of interview to ask him the question. His response was to take life easy. Pat came the Chairman of the board, "Do you think that life is so easy"? The board fell into his trap. His classic answer was, "Well, Sir," It is a ***"Neither A Tempest, nor a Midsummer night's Dream, It is As You Like It."*** Needless to say, the friend (Shibuda) never got the job. This reply is equally applicable to Intelligence. I have earlier said about intelligence that it was like "Beauty Lies in the eyes of the beholder."

Episode-18

I was not a counter intelligence Czar. Yet, it is true that I happened to make use of this aspect of IB's work than many others.

Shyamal once called the meeting of retired DIBs to get their views on improving the quality of counter-intelligence (CI) work in the IB. CI work almost necessarily involved the quality of output of the Technical Branch .It was indeed nice of Shyamal to have invited me to the said meeting. Neither Shri Barari nor MK was present.

Shri T.V. Rajeshwar was the senior most among those present. He was the first person to the right of the incumbent DIB Shri Shyamal Dutta. So, he initiated the discussion. With duc apology to the former DIBs, I must say with due regards to them, what followed was a pathetic display of the fact that none of them had ever been in charge of CI work. Nehchal as the latter day DIB is perhaps the only DIB, who directly handled the Technical Branch. When on curiosity, I had asked Nehchal who was the Special Director in charge of the Tech Branch, he told me that he himself handled the Tech Branch directly. No wonder Shri Nehchal Sandhu has been the most successful DIB in the recent days.

I had on promotion to the rank of Addl Director was to shift to the North Block. When I refused, a complain was made to Shri V.G. Vaidya, then DIB. I told him that most of the CI branches under me as well as the Tech Branch,were near my office which facilitated to remain in close touch with the branches, Shri Vaidya agreed.

The Tech Branch people were happy. I happened to have fallen in love with them. During the course of the quartertly conferences, I maintained that the officers in Tech branches were more committed and were prepared to more risks in comparison to general intelligence officers. I could say this because I lived among the Tech Branch officers. I would add that I could say that with confidence that I had known general intelligence officers in the field who were among the most outstanding general intelligence officers in the IB.

I was clear in mind that the balance of advantage definitely lay with the tech officers. The success or failure of a technology based operation would depend upon how much the intelligence officers knew about the tech job. Much depended upon how much the intelligence officers could explain what precisely they wanted from the tech officers. Even if they did not have the tech equipment required,they would devise some thing with the available tools to show the way to success.

We ensured that we could get two medals, Indian Police Medal (IPM) for Junior officer and President's Medal for Meritorious Services (PPM) for a senior officer. It gave me no end of happiness.

After more than 10 years' stint at Hqrs, I was due to do some out-station posting. I was posted to SIB Patna. But the DIB, Shri Mathur held back my release for reasons connected with operation.

MK was then the DIB. We used to have brain-storming sessions from time-to-time. The main idea was how to improve the quality of work in the IB, especially in reducing paper work in Hqrs. When the point of our belonging to the IB was being emphasised, Shri Vaidya thumped the table and said, "Dash it, the organisation belongs to us". What a moment to cherish!

Shri S.K. Bapat was then JD, SIB, Bombay. We looked forward to meeting each other when SK was to come to IB Hqrs. SK told me that for Bombay boys, the first job preference was Tata Administrative Service and then to become a CA, then get a covenanted service in the private sector. IAS and other services came the last. SK has now settled in Pune. There was OP Bam. Bam is a mental trainer. Among his students have been Michael Ferreira and Sachin Tendulkar.

It is a pleasure to have such friends! The IB has a mountaineering institute at Sikkim. On a visit to the institute, we found a young man of exceptionally white complexion. That was Rahul Gandhi. There we watched a three hour long film, covering the entire tracking from the base camp to the top of the Everest. It was fascinating.

Episode-19

I was then the Special Director. Here is an interesting anecdote. I had gone from Delhi in connection with election review. The district officers were giving their appreciation. Amiya Samanta, who holds the record of having done more districts, frequently interrupted the field officers, by way of them, and thereby exposing their, what he felt, inadequacies. Possibly, Amiya failed to take notice of the fact that the time had changed. It soon appeared that the field officers started feeling uncomfortable. Those who were yet to speak kept themselves a little reserved.

Tushar, who was the DD, SIB. Calcutta, suddenly intervened and almost non-challantaly told Amiya, "Sir, at times it is good not to know so much. Kindly, let the district officers tell us what is their present day assessment".

We practised cricket at some lawns outside the main Rashtrapati Bhawan Complex. We played cricket match at the civil lines of the Delhi police. It was between uniformed and non-uniformed police officers. These activities helped to develop the sprit de corps and was highly enjoyable. Shri K.N. Thakur had taken over from Subu, the VIP security job. I enjoy his company at the get-togethers in DIB's house. Most of these get-togethers were like pre Diwali meet or some one's farewell. January 9 was the day B.N. Mullick had entered the house. This tradition has not been kept up.

Shri V.K. Malhotra, the expert on communism, during the days when the other main subject for the IB was pseudo-religious parties like Anand Margis, et al.

Shri P.K. Kanungo was my batch mate. We do not meet PK very much at the batchmates get-togethers. He is an enthralling company.

B. Raman who was in the R&WA, he and me retired on the same day. Raman had become a big name in the US for his expertise on terrorism. He would go there very frequently on invitation. Raman's book "Kao's Boys" sold like hot cakes. Raman and I attended Seminars together in Bombay. Raman was an inspiring company.

One day I urged Shri R.D. Pande, who was a teacher cum-visionary. "Sir we got far too many reports from the field on the same subject. I burnt midnight oil on my dining table reading the voluminous reports from the field ADs/CIOs." So, I once suggested as to why we could not suggest that the field reports coming to us being filtered through the respective DDs in the field. Shri Pande explained the impracticality of that and beautifully said, "Reading through the dak over a period of time, something will get stuck in your mind. That will help you understand things in correct perspective. You write down a few lines on the shape of things likely to emerge. If only 5 percent of that comes true, you have become a good officer". Well, that set in my mind permanently.

Suddenly the question came out from me, "Well, Mr. Jain, we find you coming to the office, go to the press and do everything for the IPJ even though your name figures nowhere in it. What exactly motivates you to do so". Shri Jain thought for a while and answered, "Sir, it is perhaps because I love the work". The answer acted like an electric shock on me. I jumped from my chair, went round and hugged Shri Jain for a while. He was then a gentleman, passed his sixty. The lesson I learnt then stayed with me and I have been sharing it whenever I get an opportunity.

I was with Shri T.V. Rajeshwar in his office. He had just been posted as the Lt. Governor of Arunachal Pradesh. I took the liberty of asking him, "Sir, is it the good time to go as the Lt. Governor of Arunachal Pradesh?" He answered, "There would never be any good time for this. Shri Rajeshwar later became the Governor of Sikkim, West Bengal and UP twice. This would be a record of sort. No other individual has become the Governor of so many States and for so many years.

My happy brush with Shri R.N. Kao Secretory R&WA is worth mentioning. He was the founder Secretary. Shri Kao was known as a forward-looking Counter Intelligence officer. On retirement, he was the Security Advisor to the Prime Minister, Smt Indira Gandhi. I had met him once in his office, when I was a part of that historic joint intelligence operation along with Col. Hassanwalia, the best operational officer, I have ever met.

I was to meet Shri Kao at his house. I was led to his study room. After ordering for a cup of coffee for both of us, Shri Kao said, "I know you have been doing well in the operation with Col. Hassanwalia. Would you please tell me the full story once?" I did. Shri Kao felt very happy. He had no clarification to ask. For me, it was a privilege to be given such a special audience. My days work was done. I felt very happy. I had passed the test.

My batch mate Shri J.N. Roy covered some very sensitive desk. From discussions with him, I was convinced that had the government in the centre listened to 40 percent of the information the IB had conveyed, many big catastrophes could have been avoided."

Shri T.V. Rajeshwar was the DIB. In a Friday Conference, some Deputy Director was absent. It was told that he was sick. Shri Rajeshwar quipped, "Sick? I have no time to fall sick". He was a fitness buff. Summer, rains or winter! Nothing could stop him. Later, he was Governor, Sikkim. It is said that he had covered every inch of Sikkim on foot. Shri Mukherjee always spoke about me in glowing terms. My friends pulled my legs like this. "What "jadu" I had cast on him, that is what magic spell I had cast on him.

There was then the system of paying overtime those days. Shri Rattan Singh calculated the overtime from the time he had left home for the office till he would reach back home in the evening. His argument was simple. That period was not his.

Shri V.N. Kaul, I had taken over from him as AD (Q). I reported to him as understudy. He came, moved the table, physically lifted me and made me sit on his chair and said, "Understudy, bye, bye". It was Shri Venkatachari, then Section Officer who saved me. Shri Kaul was a workhorse. The Q Branch then was the heaviest desk. Shri Kaul would not agree to divide the desk. He was so correct. The security of the seven sisters in the North East is interlined and indivisible that there cannot be proper appreciation of the security threat there from other than studding them together.

Shri A.K. Doval had been one of the DIB and later on became the National Security Adviser (NSA) like MK. Currently, he is the most well-known IPS officer. He was AD, Aizawal when I was the AD (Q), that is the desk officer for the NE. Ajit had been, and even now, the most dare devil officer after Shri M.K. Dhar. We used to correspond via cipher on WT. He turned in to Christian and start eating meat and drinking liquor. He could take any cover at a short notice. I had looked him at Aizawal.

It was decided we should make out a case for awarding "Kirti Chakra" for Ajit, an army decoration. MK told me to give whatever we could and that he would do the rest. That he did. The citation for Ajit read that he used to roam about like a mendicant, etc. Truth was the casualty but the spirit there was correct. Ajit has been the only police officer to have received "Kirti Chakra".

It was decided to give him out of turn Indian Police Medal. He is till today the youngest recipient of the IPM. Incidentally,

I too got the IPM same year, superseding Shri D.C. Pathak, senior to me in the batch by one rank.

When Ajit was the Director at the Vivekananda International Foundation (VIF), Ajit had the grace to publicly touch my feet and openly said that I was his "guru" in the IB. It was an over statement .But, look at the spirit and grace behind. He has indeed been a chela far outshining the guru.

Let me now go back in time to my highly privileged and affectionate relationship with Shri M.M.L. Hooja. While I was like an advisor to him on police matters when he was the DIB. I was then a voracious reader. As AD(L) I had read up all the Police Commission Report, from the first 1901 Police Commission Report set-up by the Britishers, The first Police Commission Report in Independent India was set-up in Bihar. It was written by no other than Shri K.N. Prasad. It has been in my humble opinion the best Police Commission Report till the first All India Police Commission Report written by Shri C.V. Narasimhan, the first of the first batch of the 1948 batch of the IPS officers. He was very articulate in projecting difficult matter. Clarity of thought was his forte. He had highly appreciated my response to the questionnaire by him. Shri Hooja had ensured that I went to the UNAFEI, "The United Nations Crime Prevention and Treatment of Offenders in Tokyo". I had missed out that 3 months long training course by a whisker the year before.

I learnt a lot at the UNAFEI, which was located at Fuchu, 30 miles from Tokyo. At the UNAFEI, except the Director, other members of the staff had to pay for telephone calls. I did the 31st International Course. As a trainee, I was asked to prepare a paper on the Indian Criminal Justice System. I had no papers with me. But, thanks to my district training under Shri Nirupam Som, I could make the note. It was appreciated and included in the UNAFEI publication.

Our rooms were regularly dusted and cleaned in our absence by the families of the staff, including the wife of the Director.

The UNAFEI paid a lot of emphasis on treatment of offenders and the correctional system with emphasis on the system of probation.

The Japanese are known for their "*shistachar*". The majority of the Japanese work in private sector. When two such Japanese meet, they exchange visiting cards and start bowing to each other. During this brief time, they make assessment as to who among them is the senior. Till the senior man stops, the other man will continue bowing. The height of the Japanese "*shistachar*" is that they cannot say no to anyone. They will say, "Yes, I do not agree with you".

The professors in Japan are highly valued and respected. The Japanese friends never asked questions. When inquired about the reasons for that, we learnt it was discourteous to ask questions to the seniors.

It was towards the end of the course. It was December. It was bitter cold. It was around 9 pm, there was not a single soul on the road. Traffic lights were on. Looking right and left, we tried to cross over. The Japanese friends held us back and firmly said, "No, No. You can't do it. It is red light. "We had to wait till the lights turned green.

Before I leave Japan, it is time to get back to the manifestation, love and care for me on the part of Shri M.M.L. Hooja his adviser on police matters D.C. Nath. He called me up in Japan (Fuchu) and asked me whether I would like to go on deputation to the MHA against a new post of Deputy Secretary just created. I was hesitating when Shri Hooja said, "You have just joined the IB.I think you should stay and build up your IB career". Later, there came an opportunity to go on deputation to the NPA. I had a knack for training assignment. Shri Hooja called me and said, "You are on deputation to the IB. There cannot be any better deputation than that".

Back to Shri T.V. Rajeshwar, Patna was the first SIB, where he scored some brownie points before the Union Home Minister vis-a-vis the State government. It was a quarterly conference. The DIB used to invite selected outstation officers to lunch at his residence by turn. It was my turn alongwith a few others that time. At the coffee break at 1100 hrs, I told Shri Rajeshwar that I ate saltless food on Tuesdays. The conference that time fell on a Tuesday. So, I would go for the lunch but would eat only curd and sweets.

When we trooped in to the lunch room, Smt. Rajlakshmi Rajeshwar called me and showing a small table on the side, told me, "Mr Nath! your food is there." The orderly removed the piece of cloth covering the food. Lo and behold, all the items of the main table were there.

Shri K.F. Rustamji, an illustrious officer, who founded the Border Security Force (BSF) was there after retirement, working as the Special Secretary in the Union Home Ministry. Since my DD, Shri B.K. Mukherjee was new and Shri R.D. Pande had, in the meanwhile, died in a road accident near Hardwar under dubious circumstances, I was sent to brief Shri Rustamji on the North East. The first question, Shri Rustamji asked, "What do you think was the primary reason for the NE region problems written? "I promptly answered it was indifference on the part of the Centre. Indicating to me to stop for a moment, Shri Rustamji, drew a piece of paper from his drawer and said, "This is exactly what I have said, this was indeed a great and happy moment for me.

Shri M.M.L. Hooja took me with him to the All India Police Training Committee, headed by Dr. Gore from the Tata Institute of Fundamental Sciences, Bombay. He was a soft spoken man with extremely mild manners. He was a well known social scientist. It has been a privilege to know him. After some detailed discussion, it was decided to divide the report in about say 20 chapters. These were to be drafted by Shri Hooja, Dr. A.K. Gupta, Director of the recently created, The Bureau of Police Research and Development, Shri K.K. Dave, a senior Deputy Director from the IB and D.C. Nath.

The rules of the game were laid down. Six copies of each chapter would be prepared. One master copy would be kept and the remaining copies would be distributed among the others, after a week or so, writers would meet and discuss. Shri Hooja called us, gave each of us our copies and said, "Please, go through it carefully". Let us mark what he said then "If you would so feel, you can "kill" it but you will have to give an alternative. Shri Hooja, well known for his drafts telling us to 'kill' his draft. The first chapter written by him was on "Police Responsibility". It was a superb piece written in superb flowery English. Dr. Gore virtually 'killed' it as the Chairman.

Perhaps as a reward, DIB invited me to the dinner at his house. This was my first visit to 9, Tughlaq Road house of the DIB as the AD. I have been the only AD to have been invited to such dinner. It was a remarkable occasion in my life. I cherish the occasion even today.

MK, (then DIB), had in his wisdom, appointed me as the Inspector General for the IB. I felt very proud. It gave me an opportunity to know many things that would not have been known to many including DIBs. The establishment group in the Hqrs. became both scared and unhappy with me. This assignment also gave me the opportunity to discover many talents in different SIBs. There was an assistant Bhaskaran who learnt the computers on his own initiative. The process of introduction of computers in the IB was still going on.

The concerned assistant was then under order of transfer to the N-E. I was able to get that changed and got him to the IB Hqrs. and got him posted to the computer cell. I felt I had done a good job.

Shri Venkatachari was an exceptionally talented as well as a hard working officer. He was also a self-confident LDC man in my reckoning, better than 80 per cent IPS officers. Having joined the IB in Madras SIB, he rose to the rank of Deputy Director, by dint of grit, merit and determination. He also had the gift of memory.

Shri S.P. Varma was the incumbent DIB. He had once, for a change, so to say, was to take his grand children to some day time cinema show. He got a message to meet the PM at 4

pm. Shri Varma called up the Prime Minister. He explained the dilemma to the PM and told whether he could come over after the film show. The PM said, "Of course". I wonder whether any other DIB would have had the guts to tell the PM what Shri Varma had said. I have met this greatman at his home in Pataliputra colony in Patna.

Episode-20

It will be recalled that I had been discouraged by the then DIB Shri Hooja from going on the deputation to the NPA from the IB.

Now, let us look at quirk of fate. For a change, I was on leave on LTC to Calcutta. Suddenly, I found a report on the front page of the *Indian Express* that I had been posted as the Director of the NPA, a dream posting for me. But, at times, luck does not cooperate. Our elder son was doing his MSc in Physics, staying in a guest house of an old friend of mine. The younger one was in a college in South Campus of the University of Delhi. If at that time I were to go to the NPA, my family would have split into three parts. That was not to be.

I rushed to Delhi and met MK. I told him the situation. He said, "Dhanesh, it is because of your knack and penchant for training, I fought for you and got your name cleared, superceding the 1958 and 1959 batches". OK. Leave it to me. Let me see.

To add to this, Prof. Nurul Hassan, the then Governor of West Bengal, wrote to me, wishing me all the success. I had no end of embarrassment. MK managed to help me out.

The parting kick of Shri M.M.L. Hooja, the then DIB. On the day of his retirement, Shri Hooja asked me to meet him. He handed over a file to me and said, "I have been holding back this file for nine months. You meet the new DIB and tell him what I told you. This is an attempt at taking away the police function from the IB. Read the file and you will understand. I read the file. A controversy was going on from the time of Shri B.N. Mullick to take away the police function of the IB, including the supervision over bodies like the CFSLs, GEQDs and CDTSs by the IB. The file had gone to Shri Lal Bahadur Shastri.He had written, "I agree with the DIB that the supervision of the concerned police functions should remain with the IB for the purpose of maintaining national integration."

This did not, however happen.

We cannot leave the IB without talking about a legendary figure, namely, Shri G.C. Dutt. Though known for being the founder of the VIP security, he was a man of enormous talents. Let us read that in the words of Shri M.M.L. Hooja, the then DIB, Shri Hooja said in an IGP's conference, "We all look after one half of the IB and the other half is looked after by Shri G.C. Dutt. That included VIP Security, Police Games, Police Duty Meet, etc". This was true both literally and figuratively.

Well, I have been very close to him. He was my boss, when I was AD(L). Once I went to him. There was a young man sitting with him. He spent about two hours time for him. After he left, Shri Dutt told me, "What to do. He has come from Midnapore, where I had been SP, he said his father knew me". There used to be a cup of tea and biscuits in his almirah. Any one going to him, the orderly would come and make the tea.

He could start the day work only after 6pm.Quite often, he used to leave office around midnight. He dropped the two PAs and then go home. It has indeed been a privilege to work with such legendary figure. His tenure as SP in the State and then as DIG Training carry many tales. Those would be outside the scope of this book.

Shri S.N. Sood was an unforgettable character in the IB. A very efficient AD, rising from the rank, he was a source of many humorous anecdotes from the real life in the IB. His ability to mimicry was phenomenal. One has to see it to believe Shri Sood mimicring Shri G.C. Dutt dictating. Shri Sood would close his eye and go on bullet speed, that is as fast as one could speak, just as Shri Dutt did. In between, he would wonderfully add, just as Shri Dutt,"In other words". Shri Dutt had the habit of repeating in order so that there could be no confusion. On every case of foreign visit of a VIP, he would ask for a new file to be opened. He used to say, "Treat every case as if you will face a judicial enquiry. Shri Dutt created a worthy successor in Dr. S.V. Subramanyan.

Shri Sood is the proud father of Vikram (Shri Vikram Sood), the first non-IPS Secretary of the R&WA.

Episode-21

One fine morning, Shri K. N. Prasad called me up. He said, "Dhanesh, I know you have a penchant for training. Why not join a training institute known as "The International Institute of Security and Safety Management (IISSM)". After retirement from the IB in January 1995,I was sitting idle and so agreed and met Shri Prasad at a nearby guest house. Thereby, a new journey in my life started. It has been Providence! That it ended in a fiasco of sorts is a different matter.

The IISSM is the first such institute of its kind in this part of the world.

We organised the first International Seminar of the IISSM at Mauritius. It was a great success. The Seminar was held at the University of Mauritius.

The local Commissioner of Police was of great help. He had sent 60 paid participants. He was a great Shiva-Bhakt.

Shri R.K. Sinha, the owner of the IISSM, felt very happy. He took me and my wife for a pleasure trip to Kathmandu. So,the next Seminar was held at Kathmandu. The venue was the International Convention Hall in Kathmandu. The Chinese had made this hall, the biggest at that time in this part of the world, at a cost of one crore of the Indian currency. That was a lot of money in those days (2008). It was also a great success. We met Shri S.S. Rajput for the first time at the Kathmandu Seminar. Rajput, an electronics engineer, has been a pillar of strength to the IISSM. More on him later.

It was proposed to hold the next Seminar at Singapore. We made an advance visit to Singapore in cooperation with one Shri Sarajdin, who was of Indian origin. It, however, fizzled out as Sarajdin did not agree to the term set by Shri R.K. Sinha.

The Seminar was then shifted to Calcutta. Rajput and Shri B.K. Saha, my batch mate in service (B.K. died early) were to help.

After that, we held the Seminar in Delhi. In came Jeffrey D'Souza of Goa. The next Seminar was held at Goa. It was a thumping success, Jeffrey had a team of friends. His enthusiasm was infectious. He spent a lot of money from his pocket. He brought speakers from Israel—all at his cost.

It was then decided to hold this Seminar alternately between Delhi and Goa.

The IISSM is the brainchild of Shri K.N. Prasad. He was the Chairman of the SIS, now the largest private security industry in Asia. The idea of forming the IISSM was to help the SIS by way of associating some big names, both from inside the country and from abroad. Some regulars from abroad were: Stanley Grogan (Stan) from the United States, James and Raj from London, Sarajdin, Kalastree and Jeyaram from Singapore.

The first Executive President of the IISSM was Shri S.K. Sharma. He had to leave the IISSM under some unfortunate circumstances.

With the advantage on my side, I nurtured the sapling from its infancy, I brought it to adulthood.

I have talked about Stanley Grogan. Stan was extremely friendly to me. He had rushed to congratulat me on my first presentation at the Seminar held in Delhi before I had joined the IISSM.

Thanks to Stan, I had an opportunity of paying a visit to San Francisco. The price of land in San Francisco is very high. Stan explained, "The people pay for the weather there. It is neither cold nor hot at any time of the year". The few days we stayed there were really comfortable. Stan took us round the "wine country-side" we went to some wine factories to see the actual processing. We went to a tourist view point. You get an exciting view of the majestic Pacific Ocean. My wife was ecstatic. It needed persuasion to bring her back. Stan remained in touch with me even after I had left the IISSM. I received New Year Greeting cards for some years.

The IISSM work took me to places like Hosangabad Paper Mill, Calcutta Mint and god-forsaken places like Digboy Oil Company et al. I covered the oil pipe line between Farakka to Barauni, et al.

I also went to Durgapur Thermal Power Plant (the first file in the IS Branch on which I had wept. I had been to Hindustan Aeronautic Ltd.

Apart from annual International Seminars, we held several two day long training programmes also at Goa–thanks to Jeffrey D Souza. The venue was always the International Centre. It was so convenient place to stay at very reasonable rates. Some of the IISSM friends who made an excellent group are Antonio Fernandes, Stanley Mathews, James, Ronald Raymond, S.S. Rajput from Calcutta joined as the faculty. Geffrey was a superb host.

The ladies made the programmes highly enjoyable.

Goa is a known tourist centre with the Russians pre-dominating. It is a beautiful city State with very good scenic features. It is no wonder that Goa hosts the annual International Film Festival. The private security agencies flourish in Goa. It is the Mauritius of India.

You must not miss the Goanees green coconut. It is the sweetest of the species.

I have talked about Raj. In many senses it is Raj who put me to the path of whatever success I have achieved in the corporate world. The presentation on, **"Rediscovering The Future Of India"** that Raj had organised at the India House of the Indian High Commission of India in London, and the high approbation it had received gave me the confidence to move ahead. My wife and me stayed with Raj in Kent for seven days. Raj has a family of a smart working wife and four children– two daughters and two sons.

The video presentation was for one and a half hour. There was pin drop silence in the hall. As soon as the presentation was over and the lights were on, an elderly gentleman jumped up and said, "I hereby grant you a Harvard doctorate. Though there was time slot for question and answers, encomiums, continued to be heaped on me. I was simply overwhelmed. It was indeed a great moment in my life. It gave me tremendous confidence to move forward.

I have no words to express what Raj has done for me. Thank you Raj!

This presentation was later on made at the Nehru Memorial Hall in Mumbai, organised by the then Mumbai Police Commissioner, Shri Satish Chandra, at the IIPA in Delhi and at many other places in and around Delhi, including at the IIM, Jodhpur.

On invitation from Shri Stanley Grogan from San Francisco, I went to San Francisco and talked to a bunch of current and former CIA officers on **"How To Combat Terrorism the Indian Way"**. My name got into the" American Police Hall of Fame". In December 2010, The International Who's Who Historical Society included my name in the 2010-2011 edition of the International Who's Who of Professionals". Some honour indeed! who was then presented the Medal of Best Police.

A small monograph on this has been brought out with the title ***"Revisiting The Future of India."***

The Institute of Defence Studies and Analyses (IDSA) did an in-depth study on "Intelligence Reforms", Doval (former DIB) and myself were included in the study group. I had then prepared note on **"Thoughts on Intelligence Reforms"**. Many suggestions made by me were included in the final report, brought out by the IDSA.I felt happy about that.

We had a grand get-together of batch-mates from all services, who had joined Mussoorie on May 16, 1960. Great initiative was taken by Shovan (Shri Sobhan Kanungo) and Kaushal (Shri Kaushal Mathur). Shovan was a diminutive work horse. Kaushal was a handsome debonair man. This was at the house of Yaswant (Yaswant Sinha), who was then the Union Finance Minister. Smt. Sheila Dixit, whose husband our IPS batchmate had died in an accident, was present. She was the Chief Minister of Delhi, then.

For most of us, it was the first meeting after we had left Charlevile. It was both an exciting and existing experience. Some of us still keep in touch.

Well, this has been the first such attempt and also the last one till date.

Shri B.G. Deopujri organised two-day long IISSM programmes at the Centre Point Hotel in Nagpur. Shri Deopujri was counted as one of the first ten citizens of Nagpur.

Prof Kris Pillay from South Africa was among the regular foreign visitors to the IISSM Seminars. He was a professor of Criminology. Over the years, he developed some kind of an amorous relationship with a lady security professional based in Bombay. As a matter of fact, I had to tell Kris to be careful about that. It had generated unwanted rumours.

Over the years, it became that the IISSM meant D.C. Nath or DC Nath meant the IISSM. Many industrial security bodies invited me to preside over their Seminars. That was not very pleasing to the owner of the IISSM.

Then, a Dream Project some of us conceived of named as a "Dream Project". Shri Rajput first suggested that the project be for the South Asian region with the institute located in Calcutta. He found out some piece of land outside Calcutta. We could not find the final fund for that. Shri Swaminathan said he would explore the availability of fund through venture capital. The proposed institute had to be registered for that. Shri Swaminathan sent his share of the money required for registering the institute.

A friend Shri Sudhir Raghubir went round Rajasthan for the required piece of land. Shri Jeffrey in Goa also made some efforts. Goa was considered a good location, considering its importance as a place of tourist attraction. While thus our efforts held us to strike upon a suitable area in the security training institute of a private company located on the border of Bangalore and Andhra Pradesh. Shri M. R. Reddy, who had worked in the IB, when I was there, was the Security Advisor to the MD. I was on the ground where some training in Yoga was going on. Reddy took me round the institute. On return to his office, I enquired from Reddy about some vacant area in a corner of the institute. I explained to him the purpose of my enquiry. Reddy was positive but naturally non-committal. He said he would discuss the matter with his boss. After a few days M R got back to me and said that had been agreed in principle and that we should come up with a definite proposal.

I communicated this to Raj in London. Raj had earlier sent us the photo copy of an institute in Milan (Italy).We got an architect, who designed for us what we wanted. The proposed institute of ours were to have a convention hall, show rooms, class rooms, etc. The land required would be 40 acres (cut down from the original scheme of 200 acres or so).The estimated budget was 500 crores.The proposed institute of ours was to be only one of its type in the world and better than the one in Milan.

I requested Shri Rajput to come to Reddy's Institute. He did come. Our institute on 40 acres were to have a helipad. The place was 2 hours journey from the airport. In order to hasten the process, Raj wrote a letter to the MD of the company.

Somehow, Shri Sinha felt the Institute we had planned would be outside the IISSM. That was arrant nonsense.

We had Shri B.G. Gupta who was an eminent faculty at the annual Seminars. He was on deputation in Africa for over 14 years. He remained a man of extremely mild manner. By nature, he was rather a soft-spoken man. He also taught computers in our 4-days long training courses for senior level industrial security officers. BG, I called him by that name, would explain things in such simple manner that any novice could understand the benefits of the services of computers, a technology that had not till been introduced in the country widely. Many of the participants took keen interest and subsequently mastered the technology. Kudos to BG.

At the IISSM Seminars, we had evolved a system of evaluation of the performance of the faculty by the participants in the Seminar, For two consecutive years, BG was adjudged the best speaker. He out bade many foreign experts.

Then, we had developed a methodology of selecting the best participant in the Seminar. We gave him a trophy. That trophy was after my name. It carried some cash reward given by me alongwith a certificate. I learnt that competition has been given up after I left the IISSM.

Thanks to Shri R.K. Sinha's contact, we ran a two day long training programme at Gangtok. The Governor of Sikkim had inaugurated the programme. The Chief Minister of Sikkim delivered the valedictory address. In a glittering function, the Chief Minister gave mementos to all members of the staff of the IISSM. It was a great gesture. We all felt happy.

The ladies played a big part towards the success of the Seminars. Smt Rita Sinha, the charming lady and always with a smile on her face was in charge of looking after the wives of the visiting faculties to the IISSM. My wife was always by her side.

I had the distinction of addressing the annual conference of Ordnance Factories, then 44 in number. This was at the Ordnance Factories Hqrs at Nagpur. Earlier I had inspected 14 Ordnance Factories from the IS Branch. Both the heads, and security officers of the Ordnance Factories used to attend. The IS Branch background helped me. It was both a privilege and honour to have run these 2 days long programmes.

The security officers in Ordnance Factories used to come from comparatively unimportant posts. Most of them were keen on getting a good ACR from their General Managers. So, they were more interested in keeping their respective General Managers happy than on the security duty. So, I suggested to the D G, Ordnance Factories in Calcutta to discard the practice of army officers on deputation and instead develop their own security structures as in the banking sector. To my satisfaction, the DG, Ordnance Factories, accepted my suggestion.

BPRD sent me to speak in a scheduled talk in a Vertical Interaction Course at the IIM, Lucknow. Officers from the level of SP to the IGP attended. The talk and the interaction was for two hours. The participants were so involved that the interaction went over three and half hours.

The IIM Lucknow booked me for a talk on a subject of their choice. It was indeed a very happy and proud moment in my post retirement life.

Shri R. Swaminathan was the President of this outfit. He was a great soul. Often he would comment on my reports, "I wish more strength to your elbows." I felt happy.

While at the IISSM, I conducted a six day long security orientation course at IIM, Jodhpur. Shri Varun Arya was the founder director. He was an idealist and a very honest man. I had begun from the first batch with only 10 students. I ran it for six years. The number of students went up to over 80 in the sixth batch. We could not carry on with this programme because the owner of the IISSM felt this programme was not bringing money for the IISSM. That running security orientation programmes was a prestigious job was immaterial to him. I was in touch with other IIMs also. They all agreed but found it difficult to accommodate this in the tight time schedule. IIM, Ahmedabad had finally agreed to run the programme. But, we failed to follow that as these programmes did not bring money. That to run a programme at any IIM was a matter of prestige, was immaterial to the owner of IISSM.

I carry a very happy memory of the assignment at the IIM, Jodhpur.

We ran a 4-day Security Training Course for senior security officers in the private sector. Some of them are doing extremely good work in their respective fields of work. I am proud of them. A specialised course for the banking sector was also run. Very senior officers of the level of Deputy Governors had joined us in these courses. The two courses at Hyderabad and in Calcutta were outstanding successes.

Taking all into account, friends started affectionately calling me "Dronacharya" in industrial security. This was recognition of the hard labour put in.

One friend, about whom I have very regards, is Capt. S.B. Tyagi. Working from the platform of the IISSM, I had the opportunity to know a large no of senior industrial security experts. To my reckoning, Capt. Tyagi was the complete security expert. We have worked together. It is certainly a privilege to rub shoulders with him.

Shri A.K. Dave, then retired, was the first President of All India Senior IPS Officers Association (AISIPSO, liked my book, **"The Intelligence Imperatives for India".** He formally mentioned about the book in a meeting of the AISIPSO in glowing terms. He called me up one day and said, "Nath, can you please bring out the intelligence imperatives and send these to the Home Ministry?" When I tried to argue who would read that, Shri Dave came out with a classical answer. "How are you interested in that? You are an Intelligence professional. Your job will be to bring out the imperatives and send the same to the government to help them appreciate the intelligence.

The task was not simple. I would have to re-read the book to bring out the imperatives. After about two or three months, Shri Dave again called up. "Nath, what happened to my request? "Known for being a bully in office, he was polite and affectionate man to me. This relationship had started with my "thought provoking" paper for the Police Science College at Hyderabad. I had no place to hide myself, Shri Dave suddenly died soon thereafter with a massive heart attack.

This book has taken me to London. A friend of mine, Shri Raj Lakha took fancy of the book **Intelligence Imperatives for India**. Raj made arrangements, including financing the visit to the India House of the Indian High Commission at London, and organising Shri Pawan Kumar Varma, son of the former DIB Late Shri S.P. Varma, whom I had the privilege to meet at Patna, was then the High Commissioner. Shri Rajat Bagchi who had worked under me,was the Minister at the High Commission. Both were present at the presentation, Shri Meghnad Desai was also to be present.

I went to the IIPA to make the same presentation. My IAS batch mate Shri Manish Gupta, then the Director, IIPA, called up."Dhanesh, you are making the presentation all over. Why not do this here? The current course is for Joint Secretaries. This is the highest level course. But, you will have to keep your presentation to 45 minutes, followed by 15 minutes' question and answers.

The thrust of the presentation was to project the positives only. A lady Joint Secretary said, "Sir, you spoke of only good points but, there are so many cases of failures."Before I could react, a Joint Secretary from the South said, "Sir, you do not have to defend yourself. It is correct we note the positives. We need to look positive. I felt happy that I had addressed the senior most course at the IIPA. I felt happy. I went to the IIPA on more occasions later.

Shri Ashok Muttoo and Smt. Renu Mattoo were inseparable parts of IISSM. Renu was the Master of the ceremony. She collected some juicy parts of every faculty in the Seminar. People loved that.

V.V. Katti from Bangalore. Nothing of note in the field of private security industry in Bangalore can take place without Katti. He has a band friends to stand by him. We have walked into State Home Minister's house just like that.

We organised the first International Seminar at Mauritius. We received great local support from one Nishan. Nishan was the son of one, who was known as the "Potato King" of Mauritius. A son of an indentured labourer from Bihar, he started cultivating potato in the lanes between sugarcane fields. He earned good money and so was nicknamed the "Potato King".

A few anecdotes on Mauritius. Normally smaller countries are shown in world maps in dots. In one such map, there was not even a dot for Mauritius. The neighbouring tiny and beautiful country Schusses had been shown with a dot. Someone asked a Mauritian, "What sort of a country is your Mauritius! It does not figure in world maps at all". The Mauritian friend quipped, "Mauritius does not belong to the earth. It is in the heavens."

Mauritius is a tiny island. One can take a complete round of the country in two hours. Unless you are a careful driver, you can go into the sea straight.

On Saturdays and Sundays, you will find the entire nation on the sea beaches.

Hotels are built on the seas. Long wooden jetties are built to take you to the 5-star hotels on the seas. To spend a night there is an ethereal experience. Port Louis is hot. A certain part of Mauritius where a dead volcano exists, and where the Potato King had built his two storied eight bed room house on top of a kind of a hillock, is slightly cool throughout the year. I stayed with Nishan for 21 days.

The office timings there was between 9a.m and 5p.m. Every one turns up by five minutes to 9 a.m and you will not find a single person in the office after 5 p.m. A Mauritian will buy logs of wood in case someone in the family happened to be rather sick. Nothing but one or two chemist shop is open on Saturdays and Sundays.

The Seminar was rather successful. The Commissioner Police, one Shiv-Bhakta, was of great help. He nominated about 60 officers.

Mauritius was a French colony. On Sundays only you get an English newspaper. On other days, it is all in French. But, the French influence is on the wane.The Mauritian economy is now controlled by the Chinese.

Gen. Prem Sagar now heads the IISSM. Shri Rituraj Sinha, the son of Shri R.K. Sinha, the owner of the SIS India Ltd, is an able successor. There is one Ashok Prasad, whom Shri K.N.

Prasad called "Micky Mouse". Smt. Sheila Rawat is an expert office manager.

Praveen Kumar, basically an assistant bore, the burden of extremely heavy work load, especially of the Annual International Seminars. But for him, my first book, on the "**The Intelligence Imperatives For India"**, would not have seen the light of the day. I did not then know typing. Praveen could decipher my scribbling's.

Capt. Makar B. Limbu is based in Siliguri and runs a private security agency. He helped us in organising the four day long training course in Gangtok.

Capt Tarit Sanyal had won the best participant award in Seminar in Delhi. Capt. Bagaitkar won the same in Goa.

Capt. Percy Jokhi was a prominent regular alongwith Capt. Fernandes.

A big lacuna in the government is the lack of study on demography, which is the mother of democracy. The subject is not being studied at all. There is nothing communal in it. The Intelligence Bureau, for whom nothing under the sun, is beyond their purview and who are obliged to think ahead for at least 30 years hence, must open a regular cell for the study of demography. It is not late by a day to open this cell as a regular branch. It could not be optional any longer.

Shri Swaminathan died in harness. Shri M.K. Narayanan, the former DIB came to deliver the valedictory address on Shri Swaminathan's request. Alas, Shri Swaminathan was not there. He died of a massive heart attack in the early hours of December 10, 2014. Smt. Swaminathan was then at the IUC in Madras. He did not go and said, "How will my going to Madras? My son is there. "Shri Swaminathan possibly keen on meeting MK but that was not be. That is Providence.

On the death of Shri Swaminathan, his elder son came from the US. When we were talking on the suddenness of his death, his son said, "He wanted to die like that working." That was like true 'karmayogi'. I had the privilege to work by his side.

Shri Swaminathan suddenly died of a massive heart attack in Delhi, as mentioned earlier. He had called me up from Madras that he would straight go to the house of Shri R.K. Sinha for dinner. Normally that was unusual. Shri Sinha had not told me about this. He did not know that I had been told by Shri Swaminathan. There Shri Sinha had given out his plan for ousting me from the post of the President and Director General of the IISSM by way of dividing the post. That must have been a shock to Shri Swaminathan, who had been planning to give up the honorary post and installing me as the Chairman. He had shared his plan to MK, who had come to the Seminar to deliver the valedictory address. The first question he asked me when I had gone down to receive him, "Have you taken over as the Chairman"? That was not to be.

Shri Swaminathan was my bridge partner in our Sunday bridge at about 3p.m when we stayed at RK Puram.

Episode-22

Shri Gadadhar Chatterjee is a friend in need. A learner all the time, he practised in the field of private security. Gadadhar has written a book on Industrial Security. He is a good teacher. Over the years, he has become a family friend.

Dr. Gurupada Bandopadhyaya and his wife Lakshmi make a nice couple. Lakshmi is a teacher in mathematics. Guru is very helpful. He is in AIIMS. We refer many cases to him.

Capt. Makar B. Limbu is based in Siliguri and runs a private security agency. He helped us in organising the four day long training course in Gangtok.

Capt Tarit Sanyal had won the best participant award in Seminar in Delhi. Capt. Bagaitkar won the same in Goa.

Capt. Percy Jokhi was a prominent and regular alongwith Capt. Fernandes.

Bhaskar Reddy, V.K. Malhotra, Nagu Rao are all from Hyderabad.

Shri P. Deivamuthu is the Editor, *Hindu Voice*. Deiva is one man institution. He is a fearless editor. We wish we had more Deivamuthus.

Shri Jayabrata Bhattacharyya wields a facile pen. He is from the Calcutta Presidency College. One wishes Jay to flourish.

The IB has a mountaineering institute. On a visit to the institute, we found a young man of exceptionally white complexion. That was Rahul Gandhi. There we watched a three hour long film, covering the entire tracking from the base camp to the top of the Everest. It is fascinating.

Milita Chanda from the US is a great champion of the Hindu cause.She has a good circle of friends in India and Bangladesh.

World Hindu Conference is a US based institution, propagating the Hindu cause. We from the Patriots' Forum are in touch with them.

So also is the American Society for the Hindu cause.

We wish we had such bodies in India. We have a grievance against these bodies. All of these bodies are fighting for the Hindu cause. One wishes they think and do something for India, BHARAT MATA.

Arun Bedi is based in London. He is a strong supporter of the cause propagated by the Patriots' Forum. We had been able to organise a Seminar because of his financial support.

Shri S.K. Das from Mauritius also rendered financial help to the Patriots Forum.

Shri Ramesh Shinde of Hindu Sanhati is a highly dedicated man for the Hindu cause. His is no political party. You take a case to him and forget about that. He will take care of the matter. He fights for the down-trodden and oppressed people, especially those who fall victims to aggressive Muslims taking away Hindu girls and raping them.

Shri Tapan Ghosh in Calcutta is a friend of the down trodden. His is not a political party.

Shri S.K. Dheri was the head of Delhi Fire Services for many years. By virtue of his expertise, he was internationally known .One felt happy and proud in having such a faculty in the IISSM. On the fire at the Vigyan Bhawan, he explained that the damage was due to faulty and backdated technology. Today, under the ceiling, fire chambers are so designed that the fire cannot spread. There are fire walls at every turn in order to make sure that the fire be cut off from spreading by the fire walls. That will give enough time to the fire brigade men to contain the fire. It is a pity we did not have the necessary know how in time.

Another friend with whom I would like to spend some quality time is Shri Mohan Sethi. A highly dedicated social activist, Mohan bhai is a tireless worker. Rain or storm or ordinary illness cannot prevent him from producing a Weekly Newsletter on some select social issues for a clientele outside the country, apprising them of the ground level situation. Mohan does this all by himself.

Mohan is an Arya Samajist. Periodically, he organises 'yaggya'/'hawans' in all blocks of Vasant Kunj area of New Delhi. I have attended some of these 'hawans'. He also runs around the concerned authorities in order to resolve problems in the particular area. He is a Rotarian and has organised a number of medical camps, by maintaining liaison with the famed hospitals. Mohan's PR work is flawless. I had occasions to attend some of the meetings of the Vasant Kunj Rotary Club, when Mohan was the Chairman of the Vasant Kunj Rotary Club. I witnessed some of the charitable works being done by them.

Mohan at times is accompanied by another good friend Shri Rajesh Malhotra. This duo will be an asset to any organisation.

In Calcutta, we have a close ally from the IB, Shri Buddhadeb Guha. Budhadeb was an operational expert of the highest order. He has not lost the flavour for it. I am in touch with him. With friends like Buddhadeb, you can spend time and enjoy hours together.

Dr. Anirban Ganguly is currently heading the Symaprosad Mookerji Research Foundation. A scholar of repute, Anirban now writes regular columns in *The Pioneer*, highlighting the Indian culture. A student of Auroville in Pondicherry, he makes us feel proud of having known him. Anirban is also an inspiring speaker.

Smt. Anuttama Ganguly is the better half of Anirban. She looks after the administration in the Vivekananda International Foundation (VIF). It is not a mean job. She carries herself with dignity. And she has an intelligent look and a smiling face. You can spend hours with her, discussing serious issues. Anirban and Anuttama are made for each other. What a lovely couple they are. I enjoy spending every minute with them.

Shri M.J. Akbar is from our alma mater, Calcutta Presidency College. A scholar-writer, Akbar is the editor of the unique newspaper *"The Sunday Guardian"*, It comes out only on Sundays. Conceptually, it is different from the usual newspapers and is also of a high order. Most of his weekly columns are thought-provoking. Akbar is a brilliant and convincing speaker as well. I am lucky to have a friend like him. Unfortunately Akbar has left maintaining his columns after having been selected as an MP and then becoming a Minister of State.

Dr. Chinmoy Ghosh is a student of Physics. Yet, Chinmoy excels in speaking on Rabindranath Thakur and Swami Vivekananda. He enlivens our Third Sunday Bangasnskritir Sondhyar Aasar. I shall write on the Aasar shortly.

Shri H.N. Kak is a life member of the Patriots' Forum. I had first met him at Switzerland. I was on an operation. I had stayed with him. Shri Hassanwalia was also there. Shri Kak's comments on my presentation on **"Rediscovering The Future Of India"** made me feel proud and happy.

V.K. Garg, Advisor of Manas Publications, did a wonderful thing for us. He had us meet Shri Narendra Modi, the Prime Minister designate then, at the office of the Gujarat Resident Commissioner. Some three/four of us from the Patriots' Forum were there. We could have been about 15-20 in total there. He listened to us carefully. His repartee was sharp. It was indeed a privilege to be face to face with the future Prime Minister of the country.

Shri Sultan Sahin believes in Hindu-Muslim unity. He runs a website on "New Age Islam". It is a pleasure to work with such enlightened friend.

Cast in the same module is Chennai-based President of the Sunni Federation of India. He is Shoukat Sharmah. He is a courageous man. On the top of them comes Arif Mohmmad

Khan, known for resigning the ministership on the issue the Shah Bano case. An honest elder, he is a scholar in his own right.

I am proud and feel happy to remain in touch with them.

Shri Prakash Singh almost a living legend. Prakash is synonymous with Police Reforms. He has single-handedly fought at Supreme Court and got an order issued that would have made the police of the day answerable to the law. The IAS lobby did not allow that to happen and that is why the Indian Police is still governed by the Police Act of 1861. Many people, especially foreigners, would not believe it. Many formal follow-up actions have been taken but to no avail. Prakash is still at it. He has also been trying to generate and garner peoples' support by various other legitimate means. He has not hankered for politician's support. We all wish him good wishes in his untiring efforts. We are very much aware how Prakash has been at it disregarding personal inconveniences. Prakash!, not only we the policemen but the entire nation stands beholden to you.

Dr. D.N. Mandal has now become irregular in the Aasar. He was a participant at the "*Ekushe Frbuary*" event. One has to see it to believe how animated he feels when singing that immortal song. It is an honour and privilege to have such persons amongst us.

Shri B.K. Roy of Vasant Kunj Kalibari is from my alma mater Calcutta Presidency College. On the first Wednesday of the month,he organises a meeting of the "Vivekananda Study Centre". I try to attend this meeting when I can. We feel happy and proud to enjoy such company. Once a while, he comes over and join the Aasar.

Shri Mihir Basu and his wife Bisakha are professional singers. They are our members of SBBS also. They are not regulars. When they come, they adorn the Aasar.

Shri Manash Ghosh, the famed journalist is based in Calcutta. A polite gentleman, Manash is a lively conversationalist.

Shri Arup Chanda, is another journalist, who had been of great help. It is good to have a friend like him.

Prof. Sushovan Sarkar of the Calcutta Presidency College, under whom we had the privilege to study, was an institution. He was more a philosopher than a simple professor. Other professors of history revered him. On the date of his retirement, Sushovan babu had very happily said that one should develop love for something impersonal be it even gardening.

Extending further, we make it even for an Institution. The Vivekananda International Foundation, rather known as the VIF, is one such institution. We love to go there at least a month to attend highly enjoyable monthly presentations, known as "Vimarsh". The discussions at times become highly animated. The VIF is a place where one would love to spend more time

I enjoy e-mail exchanges with friends. One such friend is Maria Wirth. I met Maria at the VIF. A German by birth, she is a true Hindu by conviction. She outsmarts most of the traditional Hindu scholars and defends the superiority of Hindu civilisation over the two Abrahamic religions, namely, Christianity and Islam. She writes, even on intricate and philosophical issues so lucidly that one looks forward to her periodical mails eagerly. I am certainly a Maria-fan.

Dr. K.V.H. Padmanabhan was behind me when I was selected to be the Secretary for the DGP' Conference, ignoring D.C. Pathak. Dr. Padmanabhan was a towering personality, a sharp mind and the ability to take quick decision. He never carried a single piece of paper but had his facts on the lip.

The Conference was being held at one of the Commission rooms in Vigyan Bhawan. Just before the lunch break on the first day, fire sparks were noticed in the cleanings in one corner. The CPWD people in charge of the Vigyan Bhawan were informed. Apparently, they were either rather slow or just did not bother. Soon, the entire Vigyan Bhawan was in flames and the entire building was reduced to ashes.

Dr. Padmanabhan was of great help on the occasion. The later part of the Conference was held at Pragati Maidan. Things went on as usual.

KVH carried a bunch of open air tickets. The idea was he did not have to lose any second if he had to go to any place at short notice. He was a Yoga buff also.

Shri S.K. Bapat was then JD, SIB, Bombay. We looked forward to meeting each other when SK was to come to IBHqrs. SK told me that for Bombay boys, the first job preference was Tata Administrative Service and then to become a CA, then a covenanted service in the private sector. IAS and other services came the last. SK has now settled in Pune.

Dr. Rakesh Goyal is known to me from the days of the IISSM seminar at Kathmandu. Rakesh is now internationally accredited internal auditor and is very much sought after. Rakesh and his son had made a critical analysis of the ground situation of the education system in vogue a few years back. Voluminous data were painstakingly collected from all over the country. They came to the conclusion that education in India was then a ₹ 44 thousand crore industry. Could you believe that unless supported by the data collected. We had shared this study with the Centre. Rakesh and I are in touch even now.

Dr. Ajai Sahani runs a think tank. We have not seen any other scholar who speaks with facts only. His study of police matters would make one believe that Ajai must have been a member of some Police Commission.

Shri R.K. Ohri and Shri J.P. Sharma are our elders at the Patriot's Forum. We have learnt a lot from these two elders.

Shri R.V.N. is three years senior to me and the member of the Patriot's Forum. I have been a great admirer of him.

Smt Kumkum Bhardwaj known to me for over 30 years through the VIF. She runs an NGO, particularly promoting the education of girls and boys belonging to the under previliged section of the society. I have attended some of these programmes in Dwarka.

Shri R. Govindarajan and I have travelled together on operations. He is mild mannered gentleman and very meticulous in the assignment. He was, we heard, scheduled to be the Secretary, R&WA. He is the proud father of Shri Raghu Raman, the Governor, RBI, till recently.

Shri Manash Bhattacharjee at the Vivekanada International Center is a "balbrahmachari", currently deputed from the Hqrs at Kanyakumari. A dynamic worker, Manash is a lively personality. Once I had introduced a friend of mine to Manash. He then became a Manash-fan. I feel proud to Manash.

We from the Sarvahartiya Bangabhasi Samity organised a book release function at the IIC Annexe. The book was written by Shri H.A. Barari, a former DIB, tracing his life story from Vikrampur Dhaka. Shri Somnath Chatterjee, then an MP released the book. This was a happy occasion.

Shri Kashinath Tapuriah and self are from the Calcutta Presidency College, We read together in IA. Kashi is a direct disciple of the saint Sitaramdas Omkarnath Thakur. Kashi was close to Shri Pranab Mukherjee, the former President.

Kashi is extremely helpful. He has translated *Gita* in Hindi. We are still in touch. He is a friend in need.

Vandematram Mission is a small outfit led by Shri Jitender Tiwari. He is a life member of the Patriots' Forum. He pursues the cause of *deshprem*. It makes us feel happy that such youngsters are imbued with committed patriotism.

Shri Jitender Khurana is a life member of the PF. He propagates the cause of the PF regularly on TV. He is a familiar face in Sudarashn TV.

Mohan at times is accompanied by another good friend Shri Rajesh Malhotra. This duo will be an asset to any organisation.

Shri Jayanto Kumar Sinha was then the JD, Calcutta. He later went back to his cadre, Assam, where he had become DG of the State. He retired as the DG, NSG. He told me that the people in SIB Calcutta considered **D.C. Nath as the father of the SIB**. There had been illustrious predecessors. Why was then the special affection for me? I felt happy.

Shri KPS Gill was the most widely known police officer in the country, be it in the towns or in the villages in India. He saved Punjab against the Khalistanis, when the entire movement collapsed. The entire criminal justice system had become the worst casualty. Possibly he was justified.

One evening, I was in office. Shri Gill called up, "Dhanesh, are you in office?" He came under the cover of darkness, and, of course, with minimum due and unobtrusive security. He shared with me his experience in Assam. That was such a practical method to deal with the problem of illegal immigration from Bangladesh.

Shri Gill was indeed an affectionate elderly brother. We learn he was extremely careful about the safety of all his officers and men. In all difficult cases, he would lead, just as a true leader does or ought to do. Given an opportunity, I would sit at his feet.

It is Shri Gill who always defended and maintained that the police officers and men have as much human rights as those of the militants on which the civil right groups keep on shouting.

Shri P.D. Malaviya was the maker of the Bureau of Police Research and Development. Shri Malaviya was a silent worker with a steel mind, it was a privilege to have interacted with him. He later on adorned the post of the Director, National Police Academy (NPA). He now lives in his village home in Bhopal. I remain in touch with him.

One cannot forget Shri Abhijit Bhattacharya once one has met him for a few minutes. He will rattle out the year of joining, the missing and the cadre you belong to as if he has been reading your palm. On retirement, he joined the bar at the Supreme Court. An aviation buff, he has written over 500 articles in newspapers and journals. Long flowing beard is his trade mark. Beyond court hours, you will find him at the IIC. Abhijit has made it his second home. You cannot but love him once you have spent some quality time with him.

Capt. S.B. Tyagi (a regular army recruit and not a short service commissioned officer) and myself have been comrade in arms over about 30 years now. It was in the field of industrial security that we had first met and cemented our friendship. He is still there. Fluent both in English and Hindi, we are now on the same boat in the PATRIOTS' FORUM.A true Hindu, but not bigot, Sashi wears his religion on his sleeves with a big red vermillion mark on his forehead. A fierce patriot, Sashi will not flinch to tell the truth on your face. One cannot visualise the workload he has been carrying both in the office and outside the office voluntarily. I am proud to have a younger brother like Sashi.

Shri Dipak Bhattacharya is a lawyer. We did not know how to go about our PIL before the Delhi High Court when Shri P.N. Lekhi died. Dipak agreed to pursue at no cost. Our petition is now in the Supreme Court. Dr. K.S. Pillai, a senior advocate has also agreed to assist Smt. Kirti Mishra, advocate on record. We are not paying either Dr. Pillai or Smt Mishra. Dipak has requested Kirti to pursue. Whether any one comes or not, Dipak is always there on the date. Thank you, Dipak!

Shri Neeraj Sinha was the incumbent JD, SIB at Calcutta. Now, it is a difficult charge. Neeraj is known for his operational acumen.

He has worked out an excellent scheme for interacting with the junior officers once a week. It helps Neeraj to keep himself abreast of ground realities. The officers participating get inspired. As we feel, the interactive sessions are in the pattern of weekly Friday mornings that the DIB holds in IB Hqrs. Neeraj feels shy to report this to the IB Hqrs. It is worth emulating these interactive sessions in every SIB. If I am in Calcutta, with Neeraj's permission, I try to attend one of these sessions. Neeraj is kind to put one driver Chandan for me. Chandan by and large knows the places I visit in Calcutta.

Dr. A.K. Samanta was my successor in SIB, Calcutta. He had sent me a note expressing his high appreciation of my book, "**The Intelligence Imperative For India**". Thank you, Amiya, again.

Shri Promode K. Mishra was the Joint Director, Bhubaneshwar. A simple officer, PK had a good sense of humour to ease the tension. He now leads a quiet life, just in the outskirts of Bhubaneshwar.

Dr. R.K. Raghavan, retired as the Director, CBI. I was pleasantly surprised to see the review of my book, **Intelligence Imperatives for India**, in the *Hindu*. Raghavan is a charming fellow.

Shri Singhal had a strong and highly presentable personality. At the refresher course we saw him as the Master of Ceremony. He had a commanding personality with a booming but pleasant voice. We had learnt what is the role of Master of Ceremony. You guide the proceedings with humorous comments thrown in between. I have tremendously benefitted from him. The experience gained stood me in good stead, especially when I joined the corporate world post retirement. Have been in touch with him later also.

I was at the NPA for the Refresher Course. One evening, returning from the dinner, I was brushing through the paper I was to present next morning. I heard a knock on the door. I said, "Please come in, the door was open. In came Shri Jayaraman. I felt a bit embarrased. Shri Jayaraman made me feel at ease. "Dhanesh, you are doing the correct thing. Unless you are somewhat tense or nervous, you cannot give off your best. It is like the 100 meter race. You have to remain both tense and nervous. Otherwise, the race will be over before you realise. How true he was indeed! One continues to learn till the end.

In this course, we had Shri G K Kasture. He had returned from some assignment in London. He joined the faculty. Shri Bhawanimal had gone there from the IB. When some amongst would ask questions, both of them used, "Yes, Sir". We once enquired of them as to why they addressed us as "Sir". They laughed and said, "What was the big thing about that? Sir is only a mode of address. This is British culture, and highly distorted in the police. In the USA, even the President is addressed simply as Mr. President."

There is indeed no end to learning. We became very fond of them.

Shri T.A. Chari is a great friend. We did a lot of things together. He had helped us in the PF when we had been fighting our PIL against the Sachar Committee report at the Delhi High Court.

Shri Kothari from Calcutta has been the financial pillar on whose shoulders we ran the PF initially. We are still in touch.

Swaraj Kumar Nath is my younger brother. He was the Director General of the National Institute of Statistical Survey. He has over the years developed specialisation on gender statistics. He gets World Bank assignments and is on great demand. His wife Gargi is the Principal of Yogamaya Devi College. The couple is affectionate to me and I try to meet them when I go to Calcutta.

I had earlier said how Shri Raj Lakha helped me in making a presentation in London after he had read my book, **"The Intelligence Imperatives For India".** The two friends who had helped me in writing the book were: Shri Ranjan Roy and Shri Rajat Bagchi, In the acknowledgement to the book, I could not mention their names because they were then serving. Ranjan and self did the basic training in the IB together. Later in life he rose to become the Secretary R&WA. Ranjan was a man of few words. He died early. I knew the entire family. He had given me some material for writing the book. Same was the case with Rajat. We had worked together in the IB. I gratefully cherish their help.

Shri KN Thakur had taken over from Subu, the VIP Security job. I enjoy his company at the get-togethers in DIB's house. January 9 was the day B.N. Mullick had entered the house. This tradition has not been kept up.

Shri V.K. Malhotra, the expert on communism, during the days when the other main subject for the IB was pseudo-religious parties like Anand Margis, et al.

Shri P.K. Kanungo, is my batch mate.

We do not meet PK very much at the batchmates get-togethers. He is an enthralling company.

Shri S.P. Talukdar and I passed MA the same year. Taluk was a great sportsman. He is a remarkable conversationalist, with witty remarks and cutting jokes of different varieties. He can regale any group and keep them engaged for hours. Kalpana, Taluk's wife, had helped us in the marriage of our second son. She too is a sprightly lady.

One senior "karmayogi", from whom I have learnt much is Shri R. Venkatanarayanan, connected with the Patriots' Forum. He is a scholar in his own right.

Dr. B.K. Roy who has done the 'Chandipath' in our Puja is a friendly man. He had taken me to the Orissa Bhawan to play bridge with the then Chief Minister of Orissa, Shri J B. Pattanayak. I have the privilege of partnering him.

An officer in the IB, who has impressed me very much was P.S. Rammohan Rao. When he found out that he did not have much of a chance to head the IB, he forced his way back to the cadre (Andhra Pradesh). He did become the DG of the State. Later, he was made the Governor also.

Shri Upamanyu Hazarika is a practising lawyer at the Apex Court. He is from Assam. Upamanyu has been doing invaluable work in identifying Illegal Muslim immigrants from Bangladesh.

Shri Iswar Khandelwal in Bombay fights for the oppressed. He is a lawyer by profession. He is a fiery speaker as well. It is good to have such friends.

Shri Uttam Sengupta has, currently been looking after "The Outlook". I know him since his boyhood days, He is basically a hard core journalist. He is the son of lawyer-cum-journalist of Ranchi, late Shri Nripendra Nath Sengupta, who founded the "The New Republic" and was counted among the ten citizens of Ranchi.Nick-named, "Noton", Uttam is a brave journalist. I have spent many happy hours with him.

Prof. Sushobhan who taught us at the Calcutta Presidency College, said in his favourable speech "Develop love for something impersonal. Further extending that, we can make it even for an Institution. The Vivekananda International Foundation, rather known as the VIF, is one such institution. We love to go there at least a month to attend highly enjoyable monthly presentations, known as"Vimarsh". The discussion at times becomes highly animated. The VIF is a place where one would love to spend more time

Capt (IN) Ratan Shyam Chowdhry is a great friend. We can spend hours together. We first met at the Matri Mandir Library. We made enquiries whether we would go to the library in the evening. If yes, we would go. We went to functions at the VIF together. I know his wife and their son Rohan. Ratan has since shifted to Calcutta a few months back. When I was in Calcutta in July-August this year, Ratan had come over. We spent some good time together. We shall keep it up Ratan!

Ratan is a man of action and always wants to do something. Shri Bhaskar Jyoti Basu Roy is our printer with us for many years. He is one among such, who keeps to his words on date and time. We feel happy to deal with Bhaskar.

Episode-23

I have been a keen bridge player from my young days. I had my initiation into bridge from my father when I was a student in Class III. But, it is a fact that one needs to have the knack for bridge or what is called card sense, otherwise you can make your partner edgy to play with you again.

I have wasted a lot of time on bridge and chess. I was good at that also. The game of chess is worse than bridge. In bridge, you fight it out with the partner on the spot and forget about it. But, the game of chess is more addictive and it will haunt you for long when you lose for a silly mistake.

I shall write on by bridge from the service period onwards only. But a brief anecdote first. We occasionally played bridge in the house of one Manikda, an elderly bachelor. He said, "Try to be Supreme Court Judge. You may land up as a 'moktar' (a kind of briefless lawyer).

Bridge earns you friends in no time and it can become a passion, if not an addiction like chess. I have written about earning friends through at Mussoorie.

At the CPTC at Mt. Abu, Shailen and myself were regulars in bridge. Some preferred rummy. We joined in that also. We also played to heart's content while on Bharat Darshan Tour. We utllised the train journey also.

At the Senior Officer's Course at the NPA, Shri Naik and Shri Vaishnav were great bridge enthusiasts. Smt. Naik also joined regulars. We mostly played at Shri Vaishnav's house.

Alipurduar, both during Circle training with that outstanding officer Gaur and later as SDPO, Alipurduar, we played bridge regularly at the officers club and on tour. The Chief Engineer, CPWD, an elderly gentleman, would enquire whether we were carrying the "tools". I always carried a pair of cards in brief case.

While posted as SDPO Seramapore and then at Hooghly (Chinsurah), I have played bridge with my DIG, Shri Masood.

At Darjeeling, bridge played a major part of my social life. I played bridge, both at the club and in friends' houses. We mostly played at Udayanda's house. Like Subhash, Udayanda was also from the Indian Forest Service.

It so happened, some of us stayed at RK Puram Sector XIII at one time. In need for partner, when necessary, I dreaded to get a batchmate of mine as partner. When not needed, Shri Swaminathan and self were fixed partners.

Again, an anecdote. One day, we were playing our almost regular Sunday Bridge between 3p.m to 6p.m. It was at Shri T.A. Chari's house, I was playing the hand. In between, Prabhu (Smt Chari was away) served us coffee. I was so engrossed in playing out the hand, I did not realise there was no sugar in the cup of coffee that I had consumed. I liked that cup of coffee so much that I asked Prabhu to give me another cup. It was South Indian seed percussion coffee prepared that special way. In the process, I developed the good habit of having coffee without sugar. Incidentally, I purchased steel table for playing this Sunday afternoon Bridge at my house. It is still there.

I would play bridge at every opportunity. While in the IISSM, we had once gone to Bhakra Nangal Dam in routine industrial security inspection.

In the evening, we played bridge between 6pm to 10pm. Once my partner made a pre-emptive bid of four spades. After looking at my hand closely, I called little slam of six spades and we made it! It was a great feeling of happiness.

It was so cold there that after dinner, I went to bed with my full hand sweater and the suit on. I felt asleep straightaway and slept like a log of wood. When I got up, it was 6 in the morning.

We were at Dulijan in the northeast. We reached there after inspecting Assam Oil Company's Oil Depot at Digboy and also something at the border at Lakhimpur. I went to the officers' club. They were playing bridge. It was late for me to join that evening. I went to join them next evening. Serious bridge is always played with stakes. They said they play with stakes from ₹ 1 to ₹ 100. I said, being a retired man, I cannot play at more than 4annas per point. They graciously agreed. At the end of the game, I won ₹ 80 with 4 annas per point. Now I wish I had agreed to play with ₹ 100 per point at stake!

For some time, we played bridge in the house of Shri R N Palit, one of the senior founding fathers of Chanyakyapuri Durga Puja. Shri Palit and myself were partners, Subhash (Indian Forest Service) and his wife were on the other side. The hand play of Subhash's wife was awful. They always lost. Palitda had asked me to join him in playing in bridge tournaments.

Dr. D.P. Bagchi a specialist amongst Chankyapuri Puja on "Chandipath", once took me to play bridge with the then Chief Minister Orissa, Shri Biju Pattanaik, I had the privilege of partnering him. We had reached a contract of 5 hearts. We did not the hand for Iittle slam. But, Shri Pattanaik bade six hearts. I was askance. Gauzing my reaction, he said, "Well, there is a thrill in bidding a slam. How does it matter if we loose"? And, at the end of the game, we did loose"? We did lose heavily. Shri Pattanaik gallantly offered the money on behalf of both of us. DP and his partner was equally gracious in refusing to accept that.

I had the privilege of playing bridge with players who had participated in world bridge competition. Government work had taken me to South Africa twice in quick succession. That itself was a boon to me since I was sent there because a batchmate of mine wanted to go to the US, which was in the schedule of the VIP that facilitates such tours for us.

In one evening, this ambassador taught me to play two-hand Bridge. I lost pretty much as I hardly knew that two-hand bridge. After dinner, he asked me whether I would like to play a few more hands. I readily agreed. My horse sense by then told me that the sitting position was of great significance in this two-hand bridge. In about one hours' time, I not only recovered what I had lost but was winning so much that the ambassador hurried to call it a day, as it is said.

Alas! The game bridge is now at discount. It is difficult to get a four some. On occasions of like Dipavali, people play the shorter version of three cards game.

Episode-24

I have happened to have visited a number of places of Hindu Pilgrimage:

1. Shiva Temple at number of places including the Lingaraj temple at Bhubaneshwar.
2. Sankatmochan Temple in Uttar Pradesh and at many Hanuman temples in the country.
3. Brahma at Varanasi.
4. Kamakhya Temple in Assam.
5. Kali Temple at Kalighat (West Bengal) and at many other places.
6. Chinnamatta temple near Ranchi.
7. Banke Bihar Temple, Vrindavan (Uttar Pradesh).
8. Lord Krishna Temple, Mathura (Uttar Pradesh).
9. Dwaraka in Gujarat.
10. Bhairav Temple in Madhya Pradesh as well as New Delhi.

Unfortunately, I could not visit Kedarnath, Badrinath in Uttarakhand, Vaishnodevi at J&K

Episode-25

Socio-Cultural life in Delhi

Calcutta Presidency College Alumni Association,Delhi Branch, provided the first opportunity for having enjoyed socio-cultural life to a soul like me uprooted from Calcutta.

We organised a function almost once in every two months. There was great variety, a musical evening, a talk, an annual drama, an annual picnic, a seminar or a talk. The rehearsals for the drama were rather interesting. Sankar Prosad Ghosh was our Shahjehan. The fellow artistes as well as the prompter Esha boudi had a lot of problem with our Shahjehan. He would never read the script, resulting in his skipping several pages. The prompter Esha boudi as well as the fellow artistes did not know how to catch up with Sankarda.

The musical evenings were a different cup of tea. Master Mosahai, that is the master music teacher of Delhi, Shri Sudhir Chanda, would not tolerate any nuisance. The people of Delhi in late sixties and early seventies did look forward to such musical soirees or dramas by the Presidency College Alumni Association. There was then no Bijan Mukherjee.

Sunilda was the pillar of the Association. Dipak had organised a memorial function on the death of Sunilda that was well attended and appreciated. Whether it was rehearsals or other meetings, we enjoyed Esha boudis' *Chanar Jilipi*. The taste of that is still in our mouths.

There was time when at Saraswati Puja or Laxmi Puja,we were at Sunilda's house. Kanu, the eldest son of Sunilda and his Ranu manage the show even now, we learn. Any one coming from Calcutta and needed some help, just had to reach Sunilda's house.

We had Monojitda. He had memorised the entire Sanchaita.

Our expert art critic Utpalda has said "Bye-Bye" Delhi.

Sunilda and Mohitda played the typical role of servants. Amalda was a born romantic actor. Sudhinda and Radha boudi in her typical style of wearing sarees impressd us. Minakshi was an accomplished actress. Prabirda and Minakshi's daughter Mayraksh are expert dancers in Kathakali. They were other accomplished artistes. The children of many of us took part in the dramas. Parimal Brahma and Debu (Dr. K. Ghosh) were regulars. Debu's rendering of "Coffee house addata" is still ringing in the ears.Jhum Jhum Shirali had the best Rabindrik voice, Swapna Bandopadhyya was a top class clasical singer. She rendered Rabindra sangeet also on our request.

The Foundation Day of our College is January 20. An event commemorating that day, is still compulsory. So, is the Tapas Mazumdar Memorial Lecture.

Shri G.C. Dutta, Justice A N Roy, Dr. Tapas Mazumdar and evergreen Dr. Nitish Sengupta were among eminent Presidents of the Association.

Sukumar Mukherjee, my childhood friend, is now the only living member of the founding fathers of the Association.

In recent times, Shri B.K. Roy attracted our attention at the recently-held, highly mismanaged election I have had the privilege to rebuild the Association twice. My wife Chitra helped me a lot. I was the General Secretary twice.

Episode-26

Matri Mandir

A few words on the Matri Mandir Samity, where we get involved in a number of cultural activities. It is a privilege. I enjoy every moment I spend there. Drawing distinction can be invidious. If that is pardoned, I would like to spend some quality time with Shri Parimal Bhattacharya, Amitava (Gautam) Dasgupta, Aroon Sen and the Swapan Chakrabarty. A lot of time I spend at the Library. Well, this is certainly a part of happy moments.

It is in particular, Parimal's inspiration that we have started the third Sunday Bangasanskritir Sondhyar Aasar. Gautam has made it sure that the Mandir did not have any programme on the third Sundays. Thank you, Gautam!

Shri Rathin Mukherjee (Rathinda) and his wife, Smt. Bela Mukherjee (Beladi) are a wonderful couple in the Matri Mandir. Beladi is a sitarist of a high calibre.

Shri Bhabotosh Moitra is a long time functionary of the Mandir.

Shri Sibeshawar Mukherjee is a founder member of the Mandir.

Shri Parimal Bhattacharjee and his wife, Smt. Indrani Bhattacharjee, are a loveable couple. We are beholden to Parimal for supporting and encouraging us to hold the Bangasanskritir Sondhayar Aasar.

The Library at the Matri Mandir is an excellent rendezvous. Kakoli Saha has replaced Shri Pijush Kanti Sen. Pijush, Dipak and D.C. Nath were referred to the The Three Musketeers. Capt. Ratan Shyam Chowdhury of the Indian Navy and me would fix up on phone to make sure we were turning up in time at the Library. Ratan has since gone to Calcutta.

Among the members of the staff are Sujit, Ajit, Bappa, Bishnu, et al. Unless otherwise engaged elsewhere, I visit the Library without fail and enjoy an entertaining evening. I feel very happy.

Abhisek and Saswati Hazra are an excellent couple. Saswati is an excellent singer and Abhisek plays on the violin. They are inseparable part of our Aasar. Also regular is Kakoli Saha, who sings well also.

Shri Sankarendu Datta Majumdar is a friend in need for many. He is known to me for over 30 years. He too joins us at the Mandir. Of late, we have become very close. I was avoiding a medical check up at this age of 80 years. He virtually took me for this and, has been administrating, giving me medicines in the morning and in the evening. He is truly a samaritan. At times, I go to his house and enjoy a homemade cup of coffee. He too is a product of Ramakisna Mission School in the outskirts of Calcutta. I enjoy his company.

Sankarendu brought Bijoy Bhattacharjee, a kind of a roving journalist, who cannot resist himself from going to some one's help. A true Samaritan. In the month, he was born, he celebrates by feeding us with the typical desi items like 'muri' (rice fried in sandes) and 'aloor chop', that is a kind of fried potato. Bijoy also adds 'bonde', a kind of a sweet that will not generally find a place in the houses of 'bhadraloks'. In all, Bijoy makes us very happy. He never misses out joining us on such occasions. Incidentally, we have this celebration in respect of every member on the month in which she or he was born.

The adage goes, the old order yielded place to the new. This has been happening at Aasar. We have now a new entrant in Samadrita Borua who joined us recently. Saswati, Chhabi, Lopamudra, Samrat and Ishani, all of them are class singers.

The Aasar has been spreading its wings. Thanks to Shri Baidynath Koner, alias Bulbul, who is the President, Bengal Writers' Guild. Bulbul is based in Burdwan. A few years back, Bulbul brought a string of highly talented artistes, like Smritikana, Swapna. They are still in touch. Runu Shyam is an excellent singer. We are proud that our wings have spread beyond the NCR region.

Smt. Chaitali Banerjee and Smt. Tulu Bardah are a singing duo. Their consort, namely. Jyoti and Sushi provide fitting support.

Shri Anindya Ghosh alias Shitu is another friend in Matri Mandir. He is a sprightly bachelor. He lends male voice in many cultural functions. Male voices are not many amongst us.

Dr Gopal Bhattacharya (86) is a regular in the Aasar. He has been handicapped in his movements because of ill health and an unfortunate accident. He is full of wit and humours.

Smt Krishna Mishra Bhattacharjee is a regular at the Aasar.

Shri Subrata Ghosh is another regular at the Aasar.He generally reads out self composed poems or recites.

Dr. Guruprasad Bandopadhya and his wife Lakshmi are a nice couple. Lakshmi is a teacher in mathematics. Guru is a very helpful. He is in AIIMS. We refer many cases to him.

Smt Swapna Bandopadhyay and Uday are our regulars. Swapna composes well.

Shipra Dasgupta is another addition.

Jayashri Roy composes poems.

Anindita Guria sings and writes well.

Shri Prabir Banerjee and his wife Chaitali of the Matri Mandir are a wonderful couple. Chaitali@Mithu is a music-teacher. Prabir always welcomes you with raised hands as if he is a part of a team of 'kirtaniyas' going around in a team, singing *"Kaha Gauranga, bhaja Gauranga, loha Gauranger nam re"*.

Dr. Ashim Sen Ashimda is from Calcutta. His sister, Smt. Gayatri Chowdury, whose husband was my SDO in Serampore, are gifted singers. Ashimda is 'youngman' of 88. If you do not look at him while he sings, you just cannot make out his age. Ashimda plans his visits to Delhi once in two months in a manner that he can join the Aasar. Ashimda and Gayatri regale us whenever they are in Delhi.

Of late we have a group at the Matri Mandir consisting of D. Sanyal, Supriyo Banerjee, Monu Bosh, Santosh Moitra, Satya Sadhan Debnath and Arun Moitra. We spend about 2 hours almost every evening enjoying and enjoying.

The Sarvahartiya Bangabhasi Samity organised a book release function at the IIC Annexe. The book was written by Shri H.A. Barari, a former DIB, tracing his life story from Vikrampur, Dhaka. Shri Somnath Chatterjee, then an MP, released the book. This was a happy occasion.

A new outfit, called,"Shristir Aasar", is held at the Mandir on every first Sunday of the month. Self-composed poems or short stories are read out by the writer. It becomes rather enjoyable. I try to attend this event regularly.

Among the regulars are Shri Moniratna Mukhopadhyay and Subimal Dasgupta.

Episode-27

We have three pujaris (priests) in Matri Mandir. Dr. Acharya Mukul Mishra, Shri Sudhanshu Mahaptra (his Ph.D thesis has been complete and it is time, the final result would soon be declared). The third one is Mrinal Goswami. Any Mandir would be proud of having such committed priests.

Shri S.K. Sensharma was of my age group. One rarely finds a man of his quality of speaking frankly. He would accompany Chabi (his wife) to the Matri Mandir every morning. He will come up to the stairs of the temple but never ever climb up. He held, "I have never committed anything wrong and so, I have nothing to ask for from the 'deity".

Sensharma was a mechanical drawing engineer with the Engineers' India Limited. Once, he had gone to attend a meeting convened by his boss. He went in time waited for 15 minutes and then was going back to his office. The boss saw Sensharma returning. He shouted, "Mr. Sharma, Mr. Sharma! Sensharma heard him well. But, since the boss did not call him by his correct name, he was walking away after waiting for 15 minutes. When somehow, he was persuaded duly, he said, "Well, I had waited for 15 minutes, I value my time and so am now going back to my office. Needless to add, Sensharma did not stay with the Engineers' Limited for long.

Sensharma had a tremendous sense of humour. I enjoyed every moment I spent with him.

Among the regulars are Shri Moniratna Mukhopadhyay and Subimal Dasgupta. Smt Krishna Mishra Bhattacharjee is a regular at the Aasar.

Shri Subrata Ghosh is another regular at the Aasar. He either reads out self composed poems or recites.

Shri Rathin Mukherjee (Rathinda) and his wife, Smt. Bela Mukherjee (Beldi) is a wonderful couple in the Matri Mandir. Beladi is a sitarist of high calibre.

Shri Bhabotosh Moitra is a long time functionary of the Mandir.

Shri Sibeshawar Mukherjee was a founder member of the Mandir.

Shri Parimal Bhattacharjee and his wife, Smt. Indrani Bhattacharjee, are a loveable couple. We are beholden to Parimal for supporting and encouraging us to hold the Bangasanskritir Sondhayar Aasar.

Shri Dipak Mukherjee and Smt. Subhra Mukherjee are singers.

Dr. Chinmoy Ghosh is a student from the famed Naredrapur Ramakrishna Mission School in the outskirts of Calcutta. A student of Physics, his mastery over Tagore literature was worth emulaing. In his house, he has a Vivekananada corner.

Dr. Mukurdipi Roy is a world renowned cancer specialist. He could compose stories in Bengali and recite at any time. You have to hear Mukur's talented and graceful wife Anisha, singing 'bhajan'. Closing her eyes while presenting 'bhajan', she transports you to a different world of submission to the Almighty. A great couple to know.

The Library at the Matri Mandir is an excellent rendezvous. Kakoli Saha has replaced Shri Pijush Kanti Sen. Pijush, Dipak and DC Nath were referred to *The Three Musketeers*. Capt. Ratan Shyam Chowdhury of the Indian Navy and me would fix up on phone to make sure we were turning up in time at the Library. Ratan has since gone over to Calcutta.

Among the members of the staff are Sujit, Ajit, Bappa, Bishnu, et al. Shri Pranab Gangopadhyay and his wife Dr. Tuhina Gangopadhyay are regulars at the Aasar. We enjoy their company. Pranab lends male voice in cultural programmes. Tuhina read as a piece at every Aasar.

Episode-28

The most significant point regarding our Durga Puja is that though it is a Sarbojanin Durga Puja, ours is a typical Bengali Puja.

We follow the puja rituals meticulously, according to the Bisudhha Sidhhanta Panjika.

Durga Pratima is of daker saj. It is whitish and installed on the kathamo (one wooden piece). It is brought back after the immersion ceremony.

The family of the sculptor (artisan) are from nearby Lakshibai Nagar. They have been doing the Pratima every year. Yet, the pratima appears more and more beautiful to our eyes with every changing year.

The Puja bedi and the Puja Mandap made to precise measurement. So is the stage where cultural functions are held. It is the same Singhji family who have been doing this year after year. The festivities start from the Panchami evening. The ladies bring homemade food. The stuff get sold out fast. You will rue if you are late.

We have "bodhan" in the early morning of Sashthi at Rina's house.

On the Sashthi day, we had "Milani Utsav". We had started this practice from the 50th year of the Puja to get together the elders. Shri B.C. Chottopdahyya, the founder-Secretary came and we then started the Puja with his blessings.

Shri R.N. Palit, also a member of the first Durga Puja Samiti always came on the "Milani Utsav" without fail. He is now our Chief Patron.

Nitishda was a regular. His rendering of the "runner runner" song is still lingeiing in our ears.

With ourselves having become seniors, it has been decided to scrap this event from this year.

I take the "sankalpa" for the puja, do the "sondhi Puja" by the clock. You by then know the Puja is coming to the end.

I do the "hom" (Yagna) on the Navami day. It starts around 12.30/1 pm and continues for at least 2hrs. The ladies buy a "gamcha" for me to tie around the head.

The Baran festivities on the Dashami morning start with the ladies going in round and round ending in "sindur khala". My wife used to lead this. It is now Kanika or Sima who leads this. Indeed, it is a sight to see and enjoy.

We have bhog prasad. The menu is different on different days. It starts at 1:30 p.m and on days, it goes upto around 4 p.m.

Before this, ladies go to bring the bhog by around 12.30 hrs, That is also some kind of a drill. A piece of white cloth is held from both sides at the time, bhog is offered to Ma Durga.

The immersion of the pratima is done around 12.30 hours.

Our cultural programmes are short and sweet. Generally, the artists do not charge money. These are one-hour programmes generally. On the Navami evening, we have CRPF or BSF or CISF band perfoming. Members go in to the front of the stage and indulge in dancing. Makhan has started this and has successfully converted many.

Makhan does the dhunichi dance with aplomb. Many members and visitors join him. Pinki, who is a dancer by profession, leads the show. Shampa also dances extremely well. Bhaskar and his wife who suddenly passed away (she died young) was so involved, he dragged his wife and danced to their heart's content.

The blowing of conchshell by Tia, Munni and Rina creates an ethereal atmosphere.

Sima is the central point in following the puja rituals, be it calling up every one in the early mornings. We join her as supernumararies. Anjan's wife Tini comes over to Sima's house for the puja days. Anjan have gone over to Noida.

Prodyot with his uniformly graceful all white hairs stands all the time. One rarely sees him sitting.

Anjan's case reminds us that ours has become an NRI puja. Excepting Rina and one or two others, all come from far-off places.

Rina's house becomes our camp office for the days of the Puja. The Lakshmi image is kept in her house.

Ramesh and his team of eight boys are our pillars. You have a problem, send for Ramesh. Earlier Singhji used to do this work.

We have two friends coming in the first half of every day for collection of subscriptions. Pradoyt arranges this.

Bhog is served in the hall, which has a capacity of between 40 and 45. We have buffet system also. Those in a hurry, can take their lunch in buffet system. Dr. A.N. Roy and Tapash manage this.

We take care of the drivers. There is a coupon system for them.

Shri Mihir Moitra and Manju Moitra are regulars in Puja. Mihir's response to our mails are the product of a very cultured and thoughtful mind. Manju is a musical talent. She has regaled us with solo performance on 'Agomoni' programmes.

Shri Dipak Chatterjee and his wife Kanika are another couple deeply involved in the Chanakyapuri Puja.While Dipak is a quite guy, Kanika writes in the Puja Souvenir regularly and most of the years,she organises a cultural event one of the evenings.

Shri Tapas Sanyal is our standing counsel for culture. He has to attend to a number of telephone calls. Tapas is a good singer of Hindi songs. He can hold himself against established singers and has demonstrated that. His better half Smt. Shampa dances well and is a regular in 'dhunichi nach' along side Makhan. He prefers remaining behind the scene.

Subir and Pinki are a part of the youth brigade. Pinki is a professional dancer. Subir is the son of Shri S.C. Basu Roy.He gets mad while dancing to the tune of tilting songs. We have to stop him from getting exhausted.

This year, a decision has been taken to bring some members of the young turk group in to the management in order that they could take over the management of the Puja fully.

Sabyasachi Chatterjee (Shobu) has been the Secretary of the Durga Puja. To run the Chanakyapuri Puja Samity is a tough job.Having been there for a few years continously,Shobu wants to quit. At the General body meetings, we start off by shouting that there is a taboo on the question of any change in the post of the General Secretary and that Shobu would continue forever. We would rather make him the General Secretary for life, as Shri Ashoke Basu had done in my case as the President that Dhaneshda would be the life President. Madhabi, Shobu's better half, would possibly be proud about our persistent demand for retaining Shobu. Madhabi does the special 'naibodya' for Maha Nabami Puja.

Another duo consists of Shri P.C. Haldar and his better-half, Sima. Sima is an excellent group leader. She and other ladies actually do the real Puja. We the gents perform only supernumerary duties in organising the event. Ours is a typical Bengali Puja. There are some non-bengali families also.

Bhaskar Chatterjee, who took over from me, have raised a youth brigade, led by Sanju and his wife (Debjani)

My wife Chitra died in 2009.She used to lead the ladies at the 'baran' on the Dashami. She was universally loved. The Souvenir for 2010 year's Puja was dedicated to her.

At one time Shri S.C. Basu Roy made it a one man show. Smt Rina Mitra is an institution by herself. She and her husband Shri Durga Madhab Mitra, more known as John, as also her daughter and son, though away from Delhi now on job, still come during the Puja. Rina is at the moment only member staying in Chanakyapuri (Actually, Rina is right now posted at Bhopal). She keeps on visiting Delhi and has become so much a part of the Puja that we started using her residence as our base camp.

Tia has lost her husband, Durga Shankar, very recently. I called Durga a scholar-administrator. Tia, a gracious and ebullient lady, is an expert on the Japanese art of Ikebena. Durga-Tia would hire a room in Bihar Bhawan for the Puja days.

The bhog Prasad is ceremonially brought by the gracious ladies around 12.30 p.m. A white piece of cloth is held covering the entire bedi area during this time.

Shri Ranjan Dutta was the Secretary in the past. He is not regular now. But we are in touch on mail. He is an inspiring company. I enjoy interacting with him.

Shri Kirti Saha and his wife Paromita are now in Patna.Kirti was Secretary. He virtually carried everything on his back. Of course, Paromita was always there.Kirti played violin. Once a while both Kirti and Paromita do turn up at the Puja. We enjoy their company.

Among regulars to visit the Puja Pandal, whether for a day or otherwise, are:

Shri and Smt. Ailavadi and Shri and Smt A.P. Saxena, Shri Tantra Narayan Thakur.

The following are among friends and visitors:

Dr. D.P. Bagchi, Anuradha-Biswajit, Smt. Kajol Banerjee, Shri and Smt S. Banerjee, Partha Bhattacharjee. Rajashri, his wife and his regal-looking mother. Mayadi and Dilipda, Amit-Purba, Sumit Datta Majumdar, Abhik-Abha, Prodipto-Meenakshi, Ajit Lal and his wife, Surajit, Kalyanda, his 91 year-old dada from Kolkata, Argha and his wife, Asishda, Deb, Swapan Dutta of the *Pioneer* and his wife, Rajat Neogi, Anirban-Romira, Nayantara and her husband, Jayanta and his wife, Nilanjan and his wife and daughter, Gautam Sen and his wife, Ranen and Kalpna, Shiva Ramakishna, Bhaswati Mukherjee, Rupak Dutta, Anil Kumar Sinha and his wife.

Surajit Mitra (Who had one year sat with me at the yagna on navaratri).

Rajarshi Bhattacharjee, his wife and her regal looking mother, Jayanta Sanyal and his wife Tathajata Chakraborty, Amit and Purba Bijay and Purnima Rana Banerjee, Argha & wife, Ranen and Kalpana are regulars.

Shri Shyamal Ghosh and his wife Smt. Mili are regulars at the Puja. Mili contributes to the Souvenir.

So also does Shir S.P. Das, father of Sanjay. Sanjay's elder sister Mita *alias* Nivedita, is now married and stays at Goa. Once or twice, she came from Goa to our Puja. Shri Das gives an article every year in the Puja Souvenir.

Shri Bhaskar Basu Roy, our printer, is excellent. He never fails the date and time of delivery of the Puja Souvenir.

Shri Jawhar Sircar had made a mark as the Secretary in the Ministry of Culture. On retirement, he is currently the CEO of Prasar Bharati. An extremely handsome gentleman, Jawhar is also a captivating speaker. His wife Nandita can keep you laughing with witty remarks. Jawhar is in our group at the Chankyapuri Durga Puja. We enjoy the time we spent with them.

We may have missed out some and may kindly be pardoned for that.

"We have talked in the book how we had developed an equation between us Shri T.V. Rajeswar and his wife. They have of late been visiting our Puja pandal more or less regularly in one of the evenings during the aarati. Once her daughter, former Foreign Secretary, had also accompanied them."

It is a matter of great privilege that we have amongst us Shri R.N. Palit, who was at the first Puja at Chanakyapuri.

Shri Mihir Moitra and Smt Manju Moitra are regulars in Puja. Mihir's response to our mail are the product of a very cultured and thoughtful mind. Manju is a musical talent.She has regaled us with solo performance on 'Abahani' programmes.

Shri Dipak Chatterjee and Smt,Kanika Chattterjee are another couple deeply involved in the Chanakyapuri Puja. While Dipak is a quite guy, Kanika writes in the Puja Souvenir regularly and most of the years,she organises a cultural event on one of the evenings.

Shri Tapas Sanyal is our standing counsel for culture.He has to attend to a number of telephone calls. Tapas is a good singer of Hindi songs. He can hold himself against established singers and has demonstrated. His better half Smt. Shampa dances well and is a regular in'dhunichi nach' along side Makhan. He prefers remaining behind the scenes.

An inseparable part of our Puja is non-Bengali couple from Vasant Bihar. There are a few more non-Bengali members.

Shri Shiv Prakash Das contributes a story in the Souvenir every year.

Shri Shyamal Ghosh and his wife Smt. Mili are regulars at the Puja. Mili conributes to the Souvenir.

Sima has the difficult task of bringing out the Souvenir. She also organises an in-house musical programme on the 'dashmi' evening without fail.

Shri Anjan Ghosh and his wife Tini are now in Greater Noida.Tini comes over for the entire puja days and stays with Sima.

Shri R.N. Palit, our Chief Patron is with the Puja Samity, since the beginning in 1947. He meticoulously comes at the Miani Utsav on the Sasthi evening.

We miss Late Shri B.C. Chatterjee who was the founder Secretary of the Puja. We started the Milani Utsav with his blessings. We had his 'ashirvad" on the day before we started the in-house programmes organised by Sima on the Dashami evening.

Our 'dhakies' come from Midnapore. We never knew earlier that the tunes played on the 'dhak' are different on different days from Sashthi to Dashami.

We have two friends joining us for collection of subscriptions. They spend the morning hours with us from the Saptami to Navami.

We have an excellent team of nine young boys led by Ramesh now. The Puja could not have been performed without this highly dedicated team.

We have Krishna and his wife Narmada for the snacks bar with mouth watering items. It is a Dutch system. The caterer sales food packets every evening. This is so arranged that the house wives are not required to cook food at home after the day's toil.

We have Navami evening booked for a band perfomance. Many young and elderly, run to the front of the stage to dance to the tilting music of the band.

Bhaskar has made it compulsory that the tins of cooking oil are sealed and opened before us. Sanju supervises that.

Ours is "daker sajer pujo" in all whites. It is on one wooden "kathamo". The same family of artisans has been making our Durga Pratima.

The Puja room with the 'bedi' and the stage for musical performances are made to measure.

Our priest, Shri Soroshipda Bhattacharjee and his assistant, Amlesh, come from Calcutta. He is sincere and tries his best to follow the rituals very carefully. They make us feel happy.

Episode-29

Among regulars in the third Sunday Aasar are Mohua Biswajit duo. Smt. Swapna Bandopadhyay and Uday are vetarans and are also regulars. Swapna composes well. Shipra Dasgupta is another addition. Jayashri Roy composes poems. Anindita Guria sings and writes well. Krishna Mishra Bhattacharya writes well. Moniratna Mukhopadhyay is a well-known writer in Bengali. Subimal Dasgupta can sing and compose poems. Smt. Chaitali Banerjee and Smt. Tulu Bardah are a singing duo. Their consort, namely, Jyoti and Sushil provide fitting support. Dr. Gopal Bhattacharjee (86) is a regular in the Aasar. He has been handicapped in his movements because of ill health and an unfortunate accident. He is full of wit and humour.

Kakoli Saha currently discharges the duty of the Librarian. She too sings well and is a regular in our Third Sunday get-togethers.The adage goes, the old order yieldeth place to the new. This has been happening at the Aasar. We have now a new addition in Samadrita Borua who joined us recently. Saswati, Chhabi, Lopamudra, Samrat and Ishani, all of them are class singers. The Duo of Lopa's father Ranjit Dewan and Lakshmi Dewan do also join us with interesting songs and witty coments. The Aasar has been spreading its wings. Thanks to Shri Baidynath Koner, *alias* Bulbul, is the President, Bengal Writers' Guild. Bulbul is based in Burdwan, A few years back, he brought a string of highly talented artistes, Maitrayee,

Smritikana Swapna. They are still in touch. We are proud our wings have spread beyond the NCR region.

Off late, a new body, Srishtir Aasar has been started. It is held on the first Sunday every month. This was conducted by Kalipada Chakrawarti (Habul)

Episode-30

The Patriots' Forum is a Charitable Trust.

The Forum, as it exists today, is because of dear Late D.K. Mittal. He was an Engineer with the All India Radio (AIR). On retirement, he ventured into a private industry alongwith his elder son. Shri D.K. Mittal died only last year.

They had hired a house. Late Shri Mittal had a plan to open a front office of their company, which has its factory in Maneshar ahead of Gurgaon, on the ground floor. When we in the PF became homeless after I had left the IISSM, Shri Mittal allowed us to use the large drawing room of the building for the Forum. We are there even now.

The first day, when Deepak Mittal came out of their house after the scheduled period of bereavement, came to the PF office to tell me or rather assure us that the PF's work must continue in the same way his father wanted. Deepak thus proved the adage, 'like father, like son'. I felt over whelmed. Deepak has been doing much more than what meets the eyes. Even with the office building, we were finding to run the PF because we were unable to meet the essential monthly expenses. When Deepak were apprised of the problem, he did not bat an eye lid and resolved the issue then and there. Thank you Deepak. I could not tell joy this earlier lest I embarrassed you and the memory of your father whom I always treated as the elder brother.

Deepak is very well up with contemporary developments. He makes it a point to look us up once a fortnight and makes it a point to enquire how things are going and what improvements could be brought about the working in the office as also to further the cause of the Forum. He is an excellent conversationalist.

We have small team in the office that Deepak has been allowing us to use. We work hard and we feel and enjoy.

Epilogue

The story has ended but I continued to remain happy. 'It was the best of the times and the worst of the times'. So was written by G.K. Chesterton in his Foreword, in a particular edition of Charles Dickens's book, "The Tale of Two Cities". In my case, however, it has been always the best of times, perhaps excepting the last 6-months at the CPTC at Mt Abu. That is Providence.

Nothing goes waste. So it is said the rolling stone gathers no moss. I do not agree with this. I have travelled widely, both inside the country and outside the country. And, this travelling has gained me a lot of experience, most of which made me feel happy. I cannot do anything better than to put this in the words of Lord Tennyson:

It little profits that an idle king,
By this still hearth, among these barren crags,
Match'd with an aged wife, I mete and dole
Unequal laws unto a savage race,
That hoard, and sleep and feed, and know not me.
I cannot rest from travel: I will drink
Life to the lees: ***All times*** I have enjoy'd
Greatly, have suffer'd greatly, both with those
That loved me, and alone, ***on shore and when***
Thro' scudding drifts the rainy Hyades
Vext the dim sea: I have become a name;

For ***always roaming with a hungry*** heart
Much have I seen and known; cities of men
And manners, climates, councils, governments,
Myself not least, but am honour'd of them all;
And drunk delight of battle with my peers,
Far on the ringing plains of windy Troy.
I am a part of all that I have met;
Yet all experience is an arch wherethro'
Gleams that untravell'd world whose margin fades
For ever and forever when I move.
How dull it is to pause, to make an end,
To rust unburnish'd, not to shine in use!
As tho' to breathe were life! Life piled on life
Were all too little and of one to me
Little remains: But every hour is saved
From that eternal silence, something more,
A bringer of new things; and vile it were
For some three suns to store and hoard myself,
And this gray spirit yearning in desire
To follow knowledge like a sinking star,
Beyond the utmost bound of human thoughts.

We also learn from Thomas Gray's Ellegy:
Tell me not, in mournful numbers,
Life is but an empty dream!
For the soul is dead that slumbers,
And things are not what they seem.

Life is real! Life is earnest!
And the grave is not its goal;
Dust thou art, to dust thou returnest,
Was not spoken of the soul.

Not enjoyment and not sorrow,
Is our destined end or way;
But to act, that each tomorrow
Find us farther than today.

Art is long, and Time is fleeting,
And our hearts, though stout and brave,
Still, like muffled drums, are beating
Funeral marches to the grave.

In the world's broad field of battle,
In the bivouac of Life,
Be not like dumb, driven cattle!
Be a hero in the strife!

Trust no Future, howe'er pleasant!
Let the dead Past bury its dead!
Act,- act in the living Present!
Heart within, and God o'erhead!

Lives of great men all remind us
We can make our lives sublime,
And, departing, leave behind us
Footprints on the sands of time;

Footprints, that perhaps another,
Sailing o'er life's solemn main,
A forlorn and shipwrecked brother,
Seeing, shall take heart again.

Let us, then, be up and doing,
With a heart for any fate;
Still achieving, still pursuing,
Learn to labor and to wait.

And I also believe it is better to be a jack of all trades. That facilitates one to share thoughts and ideas with friends and friends of friends. That is to learn and leave some foot prints to others to follow. Why not aim for that?

Incidentally I have deviated vastly at many places in the book. That is, to break the monotony of intelligence, the intelligence and the intelligence only.

I have, indeed, learnt many things from Stalwarts like Shri E.L. Stracey, the Deputy Commandant at the CPTC Mt Abu, Shri Upananda Mukherjee, the then legendry IGP in West

Bengal. Shri Masood, whom I got as the DIG at two places. His affection towards me was unbounded. Even from his virtual deathbed in Calcutta hospital, he enquired from his wife whether I had visited him in the hospital. He was indeed so affectionate towards me. Shri M.L. Hooja, the DIB, whose love for me was unbounded. Shri Nirupam Som was my SP in Darjeeling. He nurtured me so much that what I am today is because of him. Shri Som was followed by Shri Satyabrata Basu who displayed firmness in taking a decision and affection towards me. I had then Shri Dip Sen, who taught me how to take a firm stand against any political pressure. He had such faith in me indeed. I got Shri Arun Mukherjee in Darjeeling as my SP. I do not have reiterated his love and affection towards me. The Range DIG R.K. Chatterjee taught me what should be done to make a mark in life!

The Circle Inspector in Alipurduar Shri Gour Babu was an example of an expert in investigation. He was not only the number-2 in his batch. He was an expert in criminal investigation. Dhirendra Babu, the officer in-charge of the Mall police station taught me the nitty-gritty of investigation. Shri Manmatha Chakkarbarti, SHO, at Serampore PS was an example of how to maintain good health. Shri S.N. Singh, the junior as also the senior S.N. Singh had set example to follow. Courage and honesty on the part of IB officers was so strongly brought out by Sachidababu. Shri R.N.P. Singh is an example of a sincere intelligence officer as also a master of operations. They were all in SIB Patna. Another example of a dedicated IB officer was Shri D.N. Singh, ACIO-I. My stenographer at Patna had set an example of affection towards me. Jagdish, my driver in Patna, was so sincere and honest. I am proud of having had a driver like him. Jagdish love my sons. On retirement also he had come to see me just for love for me but not expecting any benefit from me.

I do however, cherish the incident that had taken place at the Mahesh T-O-P. The readers would recall the officers and Jawans had shouted, "SDPO Sahib, Zindabad, Zindabad".

This was the '**PROUDEST**' moment in my life. This exceeds the happiness brought to me by the letter from the then President of India, Dr. A.P.J Abdul Kalam, written by him in his official pad and signed by him, appreciating my book: "**THE INTELLIGENCE IMPERATIVES FOR INDIA**".

Back to the IB, the then DIB Shri Atma Jayaram was an example of showing confidence on a junior officer. He was also very affectionate towards me. Shri S.N. Gupta, who was then AD showed firmness in work and afraid of the 'terror' like Shri B.N. Mallick. For reasons unknown to me Shri T.V Rajeshawar as also Smt Raj Lakshmi were very affectionate towards me.

Outside this group I must mention about Dr. Anand Swarup Gupta. He was the founder director of the BPR&D. What a quality he had. He would never give back the draft given to him. He believes that what you have given to him must have been your best. I have had the privilege of working under him in the Gore Committee of Police Reforms.

The then DIB Shri S.K. Mathur was an example of humility and firmness as also affection and encouragement to a junior officer. Shri H.A Barari had showed what a field officer should do. He was indeed a great leader!

There was what may appear a love-hate relationship between me and the redoubtable DIB Shri M.K. Narayanan. However, I would put that he was more affectionate towards me than showing anger towards me. Shri V.G. Vaidya had set an example for firmness and love. In recent times I consider Shri Nehchal Sandhu and Shri Prodoyat Haldar to be among the best DIBs.

The police literature hardly takes note of the contribution of ladies like Sushamadi (wife of late Shri Masood), of Smt Mitadi (wife of Satyada) and Amu the affectionate wife of Shri M.K. Narayanan. Smt Rajeshawar is also a very affectionate lady.

Incidentally, my wife late Smt Chitra Nath was almost with me all the time till she died in 2009.

Before I conclude the epilogue, I must say, I am neither an atheist nor a non-believer. I am truly a believer in the Hindu Dharma Samanaya. I am also a believer in Mantra Sakti. The *Hanuman Chalisha* reads at one place "Horo Hu Kalasha Bikar". What better blessings one would want. Another Mantra reads "Soranagato Dinarta Paritrano Parayene". Another mantra read "Abahanam na janami na janami tobo archanam, pujanchoibo na janami khameshwari, mantra hinam kriya hinam bhakti hinam suwareswri jatputitam mayadebi".

In my first visit to Sankatmochan temple near Connaught Place in New Delhi, I had the privilege of meeting the Chief priest of the temple. I told him, "Does not Lord Hanuman hear my prayer towards him from my residence"? His reply was, "Dikhawa bhi jarurat hai" that meant total submission.

To talk all, we are aware of our Gaytri Mantra known as the most powerful mantra in the world reads

"OM BHUR BHUVAH SVAH
TATSAVITUR VARENYAM
BHARGO DEVASHAYA DHIMAHI
DHIYO YO NAH PRACHODYAT".

It means:

Oh! The Creator of the Universe,
We meditate upon Thy Supreme splendour
Let Thy Supreme intellect illuminate our thoughts,
And, guide us in the right direction.

What else we could pray for one?

I, however, go with Ashit when he had said, "Anande Aachi", meaning thereby I am in perpetual bliss. I would put it that I am also always in happiness with my friends and friends of friends whenever we meet.

There may have been repetitions in the book. I would seek forgiveness from the readers.

OM NAMAH, OM NAMAH, OM NAMAH

Index